Baseline to Baseline

Baseline to Baseline

MAXIMIZE YOUR TENNIS

Robbie McCammon with Len Serafino

Baseline to Baseline

ISBN-13: 9781547056750
ISBN-10: 1547056754

I dedicate this book to my Mom and to all the other tennis moms for all their support and countless hours around the game of tennis.

-Robbie

Contents

Introduction

Do you think about tennis in unusual places? The dentist's office, when you're stuck in traffic, or even in church? When you're alone do you practice air strokes when no one is looking? After watching tennis do you have the desire to play immediately?

Do you worry that your competition is getting better and you're staying at the same level? Do you feel as if the only way you can improve is to give up something major in your life? Do you wish you would have started playing earlier in life? Do you feel like you can't change certain things about your game? That you just want to play smarter?

If you think any or all of these thoughts you need to keep reading. Tennis is a great sport and there are many things you can do to improve your game and get to the next level.

If you are dedicated to improving your game, *Baseline to Baseline* is your guide to better tennis. Over the years I have taught many individuals who feel that after playing for years they have become stagnant. They have taken lessons or played regularly, but don't feel like they've improved much.

This book won't magically make you hit a serve 125 mph, but it will change the way you approach the game the next time you step on the court. This book will help you play better and smarter. You'll win more matches. You may not be able to take advantage of all the strategies and techniques you'll learn by reading *Baseline to Baseline* immediately, but as your game progresses, even over several years, you'll find that you will incorporate a lot of what you've learned.

As you read this book, you'll notice that I repeat myself from time to time. I did that deliberately because the book is organized in a way that allows you to skip around to sections that might be particularly relevant to what's happening with your game now. Let me add a note to left handed players. Because you're outnumbered by a wide margin, (only about 10% of tennis players are left-handed) nearly all the references I've made in this book assume that players are right handed. No doubt you're used to having to reverse a lot of what you see and hear about strokes and positioning. The good news is that most righties struggle when they have to play a lefthander. Revenge is sweet.

It's time for us to get started. We'll cover a lot of ground in this book, but if you stick with it, and apply what you learn here, in practice sessions as well as matches, your game is about to improve.

Before You Step on the Court

Four Critical Tools

If you really want to win more matches there are four tools you must have to be successful. You may not have every one of these tools when you start playing tennis, but with lessons, plus practice, plus match play, you will be pleasantly surprised by what you can accomplish.

1. **An Effective Serve**
   Most players don't make full use of their serving options. In fact, on average, most players serve to the corners. Some players have a slice serve as well. Having a serve you can rely on is, of course, important. But you will win more matches if you can add variety to your serve. The best players can serve wide to their opponent's forehand, forcing them to stretch on the return. They can hit a kick serve which requires the receiver to either hit the ball on the rise or settle for a defensive shot. A good server knows how to serve to the

body, which again, forces the receiver to move while he's hitting or even handcuffs him on his return. When you have more variety, it's much easier to keep your opponents off balance. They're never sure what you're going to do which forces them to guess.

Recreational tennis players don't spend enough time developing and practicing their serves. It is the one area of your game that can generate the most return on your investment. As Pete Sampras said, "You kind of live and die by the serve."

2. **Approach shot/Mid-court attack**

When you watch professional tennis on TV, pros today often end the point without having to come to the net behind an approach shot. Unlike the pros, you won't finish many points with your approach shot. You should be looking for opportunities to hit this shot. When the ball bounces near the service line solid players go on offense, hitting the ball harder or at an angle. This gives the aggressive players the opportunity to come to the net, allowing them to take control of the point. When you get a short ball to hit, this is not the time to let the ball come to you. The best players make the most of this opportunity. If you don't go on offense in this situation the point goes back to neutral and you've let your opponent off the hook.

3. **Feet**

Check out players you admire, like the woman who seems to get to every ball. She appears to be floating on air. If you watch her closely enough, you'll notice her feet are always moving. Whether she's at the net, waiting to return serve or getting ready to hit a groundstroke, her feet are moving. One of the first things I ask students and adults who come to me for lessons is "When do your feet stop moving in tennis?" The answer is never! At least not while a point is in play.

While we're at it, this is a good time to talk about the split step. I don't see many adults split step. The split step is simply a quick and tiny hop you take from the ready position. When you land, your weight is distributed evenly on both legs and you are on your toes, ready to move in any direction. You take this step just before your opponent hits the ball. Even with perfect stroke technique you must have solid footwork if you want to succeed in tennis.

4. **Hands**

   The best players have quick hands, but there is more to it than that. How do you hold your racket? To get the best results from any shot, try to maintain a space between your index, or trigger finger, and your middle finger. A player with good hands has a knack for adjusting grip pressure based on the situation and the shot he's chosen. To develop a feel for the right grip pressure, practice mini tennis, drop shots and drop volleys.

Define Yourself as a Player

How often do you play tennis? Do you play the game occasionally, like once a month? Do you play only during warm weather months? Perhaps you play or practice five times a week. Regardless of how often you play, certainly there are things you can do to improve your game.

However, like nearly all athletic endeavors, there is a relationship between how much you play and results. Chances are if you're reading this, you play tennis on a regular basis or would like to play the game more often. One question recreational players frequently ask me is, "How much should I be playing?"

A question I often ask in response is "Are you excited to play every time you step onto the court?" If the answer is no, then you may be playing too often. If you don't have butterflies thinking about your match the day before you play, if it isn't something you are looking forward to, that might be an indication that you are playing too much. Tennis is a demanding game. It's a great form of exercise too. But, like anything else, if you're overdoing it, you won't get the enjoyment from it that you should be getting.

Another factor to consider is what is your body telling you? If you find that you are struggling with constant pain and frequent injuries for example, that might indicate you need more rest between tennis outings whether it's a match or practice.

In my profession, I do lots of continuing education. Half of what I read these days seems to be about recovery, i.e., giving your body enough time to recover. Remember that during a match you will use your entire body. Your muscles get a real workout as do your heart and lungs. Taking care of your body is critical to success in tennis. Later on we will discuss fitness and what you can do to condition yourself so you can play the game more often without as many aches and pains.

It is also important to define yourself as a player. Yes, your level of play matters, but putting first things first, you must ask yourself this question: What is my level of commitment?

There is nothing wrong with playing tennis occasionally. Perhaps you're the type of player who pulls out a racket only after watching Wimbledon or the US Open. On the other hand, you may be too busy playing the game to even watch a grand slam or major tournament.

Regardless, it's important to acknowledge that there is a direct correlation between playing time and level of play. One way to test your commitment level is to practice the game. How do you feel when you take lessons, participate in group clinics, or just hit balls from a ball hopper? Are you willing to take a month or two working on one thing even if you don't see immediate improvement?

If you don't find these activities enjoyable you must find tennis exercises you enjoy. A friend of mine told me he knew it was time to give up golf when he found himself on the driving range hitting balls as fast as he could, trying to empty the bucket so he could leave. He plays tennis now and can't get enough of the ball machine.

What is your style of game? Are you a baseliner? Do you prefer to serve and volley? Or, are you an all court player? Naturally, we tend to focus on what we do best, but to be successful, you must be able to do it all on some level. This book will help you improve your weak spots, and it certainly helps if you know what they are. Some players find it hard to admit weak spots. Don't make that mistake.

What is your level of play? Do you have a USTA rating of 3.5? Are you a self-rated 4.0 player? In either case, rating isn't an exact science. For one thing the level of competition has an impact on your rating. Don't get me wrong. Ratings are valuable to advanced players, especially those who are actively engaged in USTA tournaments.

Yet, I've seen players get hung up on ratings. In my opinion this can be a deterrent to your ability to play the game. Don't let your rating define you. Focus on making improvements and your rating will take care of itself.

Set Achievable Goals

No doubt you've read a self-help book or two. Any self-help book you read will have one thing in common with all the other self-help books. You must have a goal. Tennis is no different. Your goal could be to beat your competitive neighbor, increase the MPH on your serve, get your ranking or rating up, or just obtain better fitness.

One answer that won't work is, "I want to get better at everything". When I first started teaching, I was an "over teacher." I wanted to tell people everything I knew about the game. The problem with that is it's too much information to retain and not enough focus. Make your goal *specific*. And, don't focus on more than one or two tasks. My suggestion would be to start by picking one stroke to work on for a minimum of one month. If you focus on one stroke that needs improvement, you won't overthink your game, which is the downfall of many players.

I realize you want to make the most of a lesson that you've paid for, but cramming in every stroke into a one hour lesson is neither smart, nor an effective use of your time. Not only that, but the reality is you rarely need to change every stroke.

Hammering on a single goal is ideal for two reasons. Seeing improvement is gratifying. You have now made a weakness stronger and your opponent will have to try to focus on something else. I've seen too many players try to improve too many aspects of their game simultaneously. They want to work on their serve, their backhand and their volleys at the same time. It's too much and when they don't see the results they were hoping for, they get discouraged.

After playing for years, many players don't feel as if they are getting any better. That's because very few people really understand what it takes to improve their game. It takes time and effort to improve even one stroke. Studies show that it takes at least 1,500 reps before muscle memory takes over. I know 1,500 balls sounds like a crazy number, but keep in mind that if you do a clinic or take a lesson most teaching carts hold 325 to 350 balls. Empty it a few times and you're almost there. While adults can comprehend lots of information, if it's something we want to be able to repeat consistently, we need repetition to make it a habit. I must also emphasize the importance of proper technique. You don't want to ingrain bad habits.

All of this being said, be patient with yourself and don't move on to your next goal until you are proficient. As golf great Sam Sneed said, "Practice puts brains in your muscles."

Improve Your Fitness

You can easily find a fitness program online geared specifically for tennis. Regardless of the program you choose, remember not to overdo it. Many of us get excited when starting a new approach. We tend to go overboard. But, if you do too much too soon, you're muscles get sore, or worse, you get hurt and your training program is derailed.

Let's spend some time talking about why fitness matters so much if you want to be a better player. Unlike other games, tennis requires short bursts of energy and movement over short periods of time, repeatedly. Speed and endurance both matter.

If you're fit, which includes managing your weight, your play will improve. Being fit will help you physically and mentally.

Most of your matches are likely to be against players with similar abilities. While your competition may have a different style of play than yours, essentially you and your opponent will be evenly matched. In my experience, the real difference in the outcome of evenly matched players at all levels of play is often fitness. The player who is in better shape has a huge edge, especially later in a tough match.

For one thing, fatigue affects judgment. When you're fresh you are much more likely to stick to your game plan. As you become tired you might be tempted to rush things, trying to hit a winner before you've properly set up the shot. You may take high risk shots that earlier in the match you would have avoided.

Another reason why being fit is so important is this: Typically, a hard fought best of three match takes one and a half to two hours to complete. When you're not fit, how much enjoyment are you getting during the last 30 to 45 minutes of play? This is actually when you should be having the most fun. You've worked hard, your serve and your ground strokes are behaving well and you've noticed that getting to the net is working for you. When you're tired and breathing hard, the one thought that creeps into the head of the out of shape player is, "When is this going to be over?" What you should be thinking is, "I can win today." The fact is, when you step onto the court and you know you're in better shape than your opponent that is a huge advantage. You're ready to play longer. And, you can make your opponent run and take advantage of their weakness.

There is, of course, another obvious reason to get in shape for tennis. Being fit reduces the chance of an injury. And injuries always interfere with your ability to develop your game.

My suggestion on fitness would be to do interval training, which involves doing a variety of different exercises for short periods of time. Make a chart with a variety of exercises and remember routine is the key. For example, ride a bike hard for a short period of time, sprint short distances, jump rope, do zigzags, or cone drills where you're changing direction. Let me make one more point. It's important to find fitness activities you enjoy. Working with a personal trainer who can assess your current level of fitness and take into account other factors, like your age and goals, etc. is a great way to get started. Please keep in mind that certain exercises are not beneficial for tennis. That's why it's important to let your trainer know that you're getting in tip-top shape for the greatest game in the world, tennis!

Know Your Zones

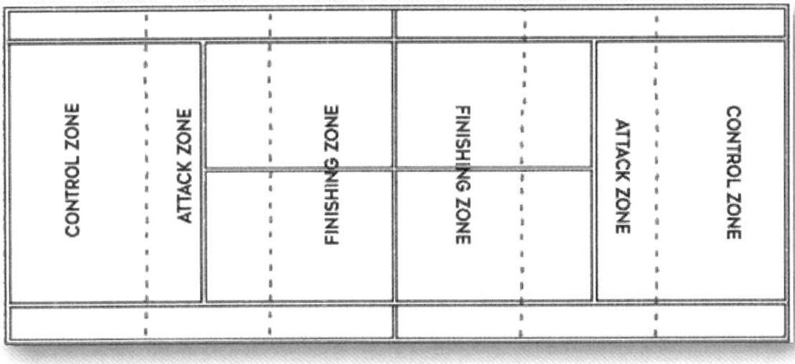

One way to dramatically improve your shot selection is to divide your side of the court into three zones. Let's take a look at each of the zones and what you should be doing depending on which zone the ball lands in. Please keep in mind that with the exception of the finishing zone, this is not the zone where you're standing. This is about where the balls are.

Control Zone

Balls that land anywhere between the baseline and the middle of no-man's land are in the control zone. When your opponent hits a ball into the control zone your main goal is to keep the ball in play. They've hit a good shot. It's not the time to go on offense. The likelihood you'll make an unforced error is much greater if you go on the offensive. The earlier in a rally that you hit a ball into your opponent's control zone, the better your chances are of winning the point. Keep your opponent in their control zone by hitting the ball deep in their court. Aiming a little higher over the net will help you keep your opponent deep. To achieve success in this zone remember to keep your balance. If you are off balance, chances are you're swinging too hard in a zone where you need control.

Attack Zone

The attack zone lies between the middle of no man's land and foot or so into the service box. You've just received a short ball. A ball hit to you in this area is an opportunity for you to go on offense. Be aggressive, hitting the ball further out in front of you. Normally your point of contact is at your front toe. Hit the ball before it reaches that spot. However, don't think "winner" at this point. If it turns out that way, fine, but you should be focused on moving into the court and taking control of the point. Your mission is to force your opponent to move, or to put enough pace on the ball so they have a hard time controlling it.

This is the time for an approach shot, a crosscourt rollover, a big inside out forehand or a swinging volley. Rarely should this be a backhand. If you don't learn to take advantage of balls hit into the attack zone, you're letting your opponent off the hook. Remember, smart offense wins in tennis. As you move up into the court you don't have the court length you did at the baseline. You can lose a quarter of the length of the court from this position. This is the zone that will separate you from the average player. When I'm playing, this is the shot I'm trying to earn so I can dictate play with offense. A perfect example of this is watching pro tennis. Note what happens when a pro gets to hit a short ball in the attack zone. At their level many times this is a winner but nonetheless its trouble for their opponent. You have to take chances from the attack zone. If you want to improve your results, this zone requires more practice than you may realize because good timing is required.

Finishing Zone

The finishing zone is the space from a couple of feet inside the service box to the net. In this zone, it's more about you being positioned in the front of the court rather than where the ball lands. You have two shots at putting the ball away. Many times, you'll do it in one shot, but usually, there are two opportunities. Be aware that when you're at the net if you hit more than two shots, your opponent's chances of winning the point go up to 75%.

What is your strategy in the finishing zone? The height and pace of the ball determine what you should do. If the ball is at or above your shoulder, be aggressive, hitting hard and down on the ball. If the ball is below your shoulder, think more about placement and taking pace off the ball. Angles are a must in this zone and they should be easier to accomplish here as opposed to the other zones because you will be closer to the net. It's worth noting that in the finishing zone you'll win more points using angles with less pace than you will with power. It's not as gratifying, perhaps, but its smart tennis.

You should also learn to change gears, alternating between hitting the ball hard and soft in this zone. For example, if you hit a hard shot at a player who is standing at the baseline and they return it, your next shot should be soft, forcing your adversary to run. Remember you just hit a ball with pace so they are usually back in the court. Touch shots may not be as fun, but I love to see my opponent run as fast as they can, knowing that they're never going to get to the ball in time.

Racket Head Speed: What's Your Number?

The average player who watches the pros hit on television sees how hard these players hit the ball. They're tempted to imitate the pros hoping to get better results. They wind up swinging too hard and it doesn't work. What they don't know is that players like Djokovic, Nadal and Serena Williams can hit the ball a lot harder than they do in matches. They know the speed that works best for them. Too many recreational players want to swing at number 9 or 10 but in doing so; they give up accuracy and control, thus committing avoidable unforced errors.

How fast are you swinging your racket on forehands and backhands? One of my favorite exercises with students is to have them hit ten balls where swinging as softly as possible is number 1 and swinging as hard as possible is number 10. By the time they hit balls at numbers 6, 7 and 8, they have found their sweet spot. After that, the balls go long and some players even lose their balance.

My first teacher taught me the importance of balance this way: He had me hold a cup of water, ¾ full, in my non-dominant hand while I hit forehands. The goal is to swing your racket as hard as you can while maintaining *balance and control.* In other words, when your stroke is completed, if you are leaning left or right and/or your foot is off the ground, you're swinging too hard. Once you find your number, or sweet spot, stay with it even if you miss a few. Don't be in a hurry to make an adjustment. With patience you will give your body a chance to develop muscle memory.

I should point out that spin is a factor in determining what your best number is. The more topspin you can impart, the harder you can swing because the ball will sink faster and stay in the court more often.

When it comes to determining your ideal backhand number, keep in mind that if you have a two-handed backhand, you might be able to swing one number higher than you do with your forehand because you are striking the ball using your non-dominant hand and there is little touch involved. Conversely, if you have a one-handed backhand, your swing number should be one less than your forehand number since one of the benefits of the one-handed backhand is placement.

Some recreational tennis players are prone to adjusting their swing when they start to miss a few balls. They get tentative; they shorten their swing, dropping their number to 4 or 5, believing they're playing it safe. They start playing not to lose rather than to win. Other players swing harder when they're not hitting the ball well, perhaps due to nerves or frustration. In reality, you'll get better results if you stick to your number.

Which Racket is Right for You?

One question I am frequently asked is, "When should I buy a new racket?" Rackets can last for years. I've taught players who simply love their 20 year old rackets. However, tennis rackets can and do lose their performance characteristics. Technology is always advancing as well. Materials manufacturers use to make rackets and head size options change with the times.

It's quite possible that a new racket will improve your performance. The bottom line: Buy a new racket when you are no longer getting the pace or control you were getting when you bought your current racket.

The key factors in choosing a racket are; weight, balance, head size, length, grip size and string pattern. Let's have a look at each and see what might make sense for you.

Weight

I recommend you play with a racket as heavy as you can handle. A heavier racket allows you to swing all the way through. Too light a racket may send the ball sailing. One of the long term advantages of playing with a heavier racket is that it typically flexes more than a lighter racket, which is easier on your arm and offers better touch. This is not to say that you have to play with a 12 ounce racket of course. On the other hand, not many of you should be playing with a 9 ounce racket. A lighter racket with its stiffer frame will likely put more stress on your arm which could lead to tennis elbow. One ounce in a tennis racket is significant. Remember that you will swing your racket hundreds of times in a match.

Balance

Balance is how the weight is distributed in the frame. Most rackets are either head heavy or head light, but some manufacturers do make an even balanced frame. Head heavy typically tends to increase racket head speed. Head light works better for players who are good at creating their own racket head speed and need better control. When you demo a new racket, try both. The one that allows you better control is right for you.

Head size

Rackets today range from 85 to 137 square inches. Generally, the larger the head size, the more power you have. I recommend a smaller head size if you want to emphasize control and maneuverability. A smaller head size usually affords better racket control. The typical range in racket head sizes runs from 95 to 110 square inches. If you're playing with a 110 square inches, consider trying a 107 or even a 105. How much difference do you see in power? If you have to abbreviate your stroke or add excessive spin to keep the ball in the court then look into a smaller head size.

Length

The standard length of a tennis racket is 27 inches. Many manufacturers offer 27 ¼ and 27 ½ inch rackets too. Longer rackets tend to generate more pace, thanks to the added leverage the extra ¼ to ½ inches provides. While this is great for serving, longer rackets aren't user friendly for ground strokes or net play, because preparation is more difficult and you need stronger wrists. Most touring pros use a 27" racket.

Grip Size

Choosing a grip size is one of the most important equipment related decisions you will make. Larger grip sizes generate more power while smaller sizes make it easier to generate more spin. Select a grip that's too small and you are more prone to tennis elbow. A player like Rafael Nadal can get away with a smaller grip because he has the strength and conditioning to handle it. Ideally you want to be able to get your index finger between the tips of your racket hand fingers and the base and heal of your thumb. If your racket is turning in your hand, the grip is too big.

One more thing you should consider in choosing the best racket for you is the importance of testing your choice before you buy. Don't fall in love at first sight! Play at least two matches before you buy it. Pay attention to the strings in your demo racket too. Are they right for you? How old are they? The strings in your demo racket can mislead you regarding the new racket's performance. You may want to consider restringing the demo with your favorite strings before you play. That will give you a much better idea of whether the racket is right for you.

Find Your Ideal Strings

Tennis lovers are always looking for any way they can find to improve their game, but I wonder how many really understand how important their strings are. The strings you choose can make a huge difference in your game in terms of power, control and spin. Yet, there are so many different types of string to choose from that it can be overwhelming. I recommend that you experiment with different strings to see what works best for your style of play.

I love tennis gear whether it's the racket or the strings. I'm always interested in the latest advances. I don't know if it's a guy thing or it's just me being a tennis buff, but I love to try new things. I'm going to make this as simple as possible. Your local pro should be able to point you in the right direction.

1. **Polyester**

   "Poly" strings are for aggressive swingers who need added spin to help them control their strokes. Poly strings are one solid piece of string that can have an edged shape that rebounds well after the ball has been hit, thus giving them more spin factor. These strings are typically much stiffer than others and are usually strung at least 5lbs less than other string types. These strings are usually great for durability but tend to lose tension faster than others. I would recommend using these in the mains only and putting a synthetic gut, natural gut or multifilament in the crosses to help maintain tension and reduce wear and tear on your arm. If you have no elbow problems or a racket with a very open pattern, you could use all poly and no hybrid. Even though many manufacturers offer softer versions of these strings, anyone with elbow problems should stay away from them. If you choose poly, be sure to have it strung at 5 pounds less than other string types.

By the way, while polyester strings are used primarily for control, some are designed for power.

2. **Co-poly**

   Co-poly strings are the latest and greatest in the polyester world. These strings are enhanced with other materials to make them softer. They are easier on the arm and maintain tension longer. They are great for experienced players who want the spin and control but also need more feel or touch.

3. **Multifilament**

   These strings have hundreds of fibers woven together to give you a softer string with more feel. The intention is to simulate natural gut. These strings can be pricey, but they provide great elasticity and reduce the shock when you hit the ball. These strings are for players looking for more feel and power, or for those who have elbow problems. These strings are *not* for string breakers. These are very comfortable strings that do tend to fray a little, but that does not always mean they are getting ready to break.

4. **Synthetic Gut**

   The old stand by. Synthetic gut has been around for years and is constructed from man-made fibers. Typically made with one or two strands, they are very cost effective. Synthetic gut also maintains tension fairly well and is a little stiffer than a multifilament but not as stiff as a poly. Most manufacturers make a synthetic gut and they can come in many variations. Some strings are smooth; some will have grooves or even raised strains to aide with topspin. These strings come in a wide selection of colors and are great for those who don't play every week since they maintain tension and buying them won't break the bank. Many players like to use these strings in the crosses of a hybrid to help maintain tension.

5. **Natural Gut**
   The "Grand Daddy" of them all. Natural gut has been around since the beginning and is still used today, especially on tour. This may seem a little gross, but most gut is made from cow or sheep intestine. Gut offers the best feel. Contrary to popular belief, if it's high quality, it maintains its tension extremely well. And, it's more durable than one might think. If you are going to string your racket with gut, I suggest that you take it to a very experienced stringer because if done in haste, it will affect its durability. Natural gut is very expensive, but if you are a tennis enthusiast, I highly recommend trying gut at some point and time.

Hybrid Pattern

Many tennis players string their rackets with two different kinds of strings. This is known as a hybrid, meaning you use one type of string in the mains and another in the crosses. Roger Federer plays with a poly in the mains and natural gut in the crosses. In doing so, he achieves power and spin from the poly strings and great feel and the desired tension maintenance with gut in the crosses. There are multiple choices with a hybrid, of course. Discuss with your pro what might work best for you.

Please keep in mind that when it comes to stringing, you should experiment with different tensions and string types to give you more playing options. If you're lucky enough to have two or more identical rackets and you're not a "string breaker" you may want to have a power racket and a control racket. You can do this by stringing one racket at a lower tension for more power and the other one at a higher tension for more control.

Which racket should you use? If you're playing in cooler weather, or your opponent doesn't generate much pace, you may want more power. If you're playing someone who has more power than you do, you may want to use the racket that offers more control.

Now, what about restringing your racket? First of all, when do you re-string? The old stand by for years has been however many times you play a week are how many times a year you string your racket. I'm not a fan of this "rule," simply because some people hit with more pace than others and some use more spin, causing more wear or tension loss.

Also, it makes a difference what string you currently have in your racket. Some strings hold tension for a longer period than other types of string. So, when should you re-string? It's time to restring when your shots lack control or power. If shots you normally hit are going long or seem a bit wild when trying to hit your selected targets chances are you've lost a good bit of tension and it's time to restring. If you are missing that pop on your serve that you had a month ago or your ground strokes seem less powerful than before, it's time to restring.

Here are the most important string characteristics, their benefits and who should consider them.

Gauge

Most players do at least some research on the type of string they're considering, but not as many pay much attention to the gauge. Gauge refers to the thickness of the string. Most strings are offered in a variety of gauges. The most common gauges are 17, 16 and 15, the higher the number, the thinner the string. Some might also see a higher number than 17 or L next to the gauge and all that means is it is a light version. For example 15L would mean that it's thinner than a 15 but not quite as thin as a 16. The standard gauge is 16, but if you are not a chronic string breaker, then I would suggest 17 gauge. A thin string will give you more feel and pop, but it will not last as long as a 16 or 15.

Tension

String tension is very important. The tension of your strings simply refers to how tightly your racket's been strung. Once you find the string you prefer, you might want to try different tensions. The only way to do this is to try playing with it to see if you are getting the results you want. The first place to start is by looking at your racket and seeing what range the manufacturer suggests. Many players start in the middle of the range and adjust from there. If you are looking for power you will string it on the lower end of the range. If it's control you want, you will take it up a few pounds to the higher end of the range. Tension is a matter of preference. It might be a good idea to document the tension after you have it strung so you can adjust if needed. If you experience elbow issues, I recommend softer strings, strung on the lower end of the scale.

What is Your Racket Telling You?

Have you ever taken a close look at your racket? Many players don't. Examining the wear on your racket can give you vital information about your game. Get your racket and look at the bumper guard. Is it wearing at 12 o'clock? How about equally at 11 and 1? If your bumper guard is wearing at 12 o'clock, this could mean that you aren't using a true continental grip when you are going for low volleys, or low balls in general. You are using more of an Eastern forehand grip. If you are not using a continental grip for low balls then the face of the racket won't open as much and you won't have as much success. If your bumper guard wear is at 11 and 1, that's a good thing. Just be sure to replace your guard once it starts to wear to the graphite, or you risk cracking, or even breaking, your racket.

Now look at your grip. Is the grip worn evenly or are there certain areas wearing more quickly? Grip pressure is vital to your game since it constantly changes due to the pace, or lack of pace, you are trying to put on the ball. If your grip is wearing out in the area where you place your thumb it's normal. The thumb provides a good deal of pressure and your other finger should loosen up as you are hitting the ball. If you have a two-handed backhand check to see if there is any wear at the top of your grip. In tennis, there is no shot in which you should be giving it a "death grip," but there should be a little wear at the top your grip to note that you are using your non-dominant hand for your backhand.

Does your frame have large chips or chunks of paint missing? If this is the case, stop getting so mad and quit abusing your racket. All kidding aside, little things do make a difference. Take notice of you racket because seemingly small things can add up to a big difference in your game.

How to Watch Professional Tennis

Can you improve your game by watching the pros play? According to Patrick Mouratoglou, who at the time this was written was Serena Williams's coach, you can. "When you see people doing the right thing all the time or most of the time, it comes into your head and then you do it more naturally," he said. "I know a lot of people who improved just by watching. That's a great way to learn, because you don't think, you just copy, without trying."

What specifically should you look for?

- Notice serve placement; variety, pace, and spin.
- Professional tennis players rarely display their emotions. When things are not going well, they hide their disappointment at a bad shot or a bad line call. They remain focused on the next point and they don't encourage their opponents by showing them they are upset.
- Watch footwork. On average how many steps does a pro take per shot? In singles its 12-16 steps. The closer a pro gets to take the shot, the shorter the steps.

- Notice their decision making process. For example, when do they change the ball's direction? Sometimes they are patient. Other times aggressive. What's going on during these moments?
- What do they do on changeovers?
- What game plan adjustments do they make?

Notice these aspects of the game and then apply them to your game. In addition to learning, I hope watching professionals inspires you to get out and play some tennis.

Find the Right Pro for You

If you've played the game for a while, you know there is a lot more to tennis than meets the eye. While I'm sure most of you have a full plate, with family and work responsibilities, the more often you take lessons from your local tennis professional the better off you'll be. You might be too busy to take lessons regularly, but even an occasional lesson can be very rewarding. Smart players set goals for themselves. When you set your next goal it's important to meet with a tennis pro who can lead you step by step to the best way to achieve your goal. A pro will work with you on proper technique and practice routines.

If you're new to the game of tennis, the first thing you'll want to do is find a pro you are comfortable working with. You can use a search engine on the Web to find local pros who are offering lessons. Tennis shops and private clubs are also sources for this type of information. Look for a USPTA or PTR certified professional. Don't be afraid to ask around. For example, pros affiliated with private clubs often give lessons to non-members. Take a lesson from a pro to see how it goes. Remember, you're not getting married. You don't even have to sign up for a year's worth of lessons. You want a pro who matches your personality, someone whose teaching style complements the way you prefer to learn.

There are many styles of teaching tennis, but in general, I have found there are three types to choose from.

The Technician

This is the pro that insists that you do everything in a technically correct manner. You probably won't get much of a cardio workout during your lesson, and it may not be as much fun as lessons you might get elsewhere. However, if you're a beginner or someone who wants to make a major change to your game, this is the pro for you.

The Cardio Pro

Want a great workout? Look for a cardio pro. This pro will feed you a lot of balls, moving you to different parts of the court. You will get a high energy workout, but instruction is not the primary focus. The cardio pro is great for players who regard tennis as a source of exercise. If you've been playing for a few years and your footwork needs improvement, or you want to build your stamina, this is the instructor for you.

The Drill Sargent

Some tennis pros try to motivate players by yelling at them, constantly pointing out errors. In fact, some players actually say they want their pro to yell at them. Yelling tends to focus on negative feedback, which usually breeds worse performance rather than improvement. Some players feel this approach motivates them. If that's you, this is the pro for you.

Three things that will help you get the most out of working with a pro:

1. Find a pro that fits your personality.
2. Look forward to every lesson. Come prepared to learn something new and iron out flaws.
3. Honestly assess your progress over time. If you're working at it and your game isn't improving, move on.

Find the Right Partner for You

Whether you are a doubles player or simply looking for someone to practice with, it's very important to find the right partner. Working with someone you get along with, someone whose skills you respect and whose skills complement, rather than match yours, will allow you to improve your game and your match results. For example, if you are an aggressive player, find a partner who is a solid player but less of a risk taker.

Relative skill level is also an important factor. Ideally, you should be evenly matched. However, it is also to your advantage if your partner is a bit better than you are. That's certainly one way to elevate your game. Of course there are limits. If you are say a 4.0 player and your hitting partner is a 3.0 player, you may both become frustrated. When it comes to having a regular partner, I strongly recommend that you find someone not more than one level above or below yours. It's okay too if you are the stronger player on your team. Just make sure that your partner isn't holding you back from performing up to your potential.

Speaking of performance, look for a partner whose fitness level matches yours. One of the most frustrating experiences you will have on the tennis court occurs when one of you is just getting revved-up while the other is fading.

When seeking a doubles partner, personality is every bit as important as complementary styles of play. You want a partner who really is a team player. A good partner is supportive at all times, especially when things aren't going well. A partner who has a way of expressing disappointment when you miss an easy shot, or double fault, either verbally or non-verbally, is not someone you should invest time in. A good partner wants to win as much as you do and is interested in improving her game...and yours. It's critical that you both commit to working on your game. Otherwise, you will become stagnant as a team and soon find yourself looking for a new partner.

Finding a suitable partner that happens to hit left handed (assuming you're a righty) is another plus. As Bob and Mike Bryan, winners of many grand slam tournaments have clearly demonstrated, having two forehands to cover the middle of the court works.

Finally, let's not forget the importance of logistics. It helps if your partner lives close by, so getting together isn't a problem because of the distance between you. The same can be said for schedules. If you and your partner are usually available on the same days and times, that is also a plus.

Wanted: Doubles Partner

One question I hear frequently, even from students who have been playing a while is, "What exactly is my role in the different positions when I play doubles?" If I were to run an ad for a tennis partner it might look something like this:

Experienced tennis player seeks doubles partner to enter and win matches. Successful applicant will be a skilled server, returner and net player. Must also have a positive, encouraging attitude and be able to adapt to multiple playing styles. If you have demonstrated the following specific qualifications, please apply ASAP."

The job description:

The server must be:

- Able to consistently get the point started at a level sufficient to allow us to dictate each point.
- Prepared to inform your partner of the type of serve and its intended location.
- Willing and able to come to the net.
- Prepared to switch from one side of the court to the other if your partner poaches.
- Ready to handle lobs over your partner's head.

The server's net person must:

- Know where your partner plans to serve and act accordingly.
- Be prepared to poach, especially a return of serve.
- Be prepared to utilize the Australian and/or the I formation.

The returner must be:

- Able to consistently get the ball back in play away from the opposition's net player.
- Willing and able to advance to the net.
- Be prepared to handle lobs over your partner's head.

The returner's net person must be:

- Able to pick up on your partner's return and be ready to move in the right direction.
- Able to get your racket on the ball early in the rally to give your partner the opportunity to come to the net.
- Prepared to make line calls on serve.

Obviously, like most job descriptions, this one describes the perfect candidate. Perfection isn't the goal, but finding a partner who can handle his or her duties is a must.

Pre-Match

Do You Have a Ritual?

Let's say you have a match this afternoon or this evening. What do you do to get ready? Most touring tennis professionals have a ritual they follow to help them get mentally and physically ready for the match. Rafael Nadal always takes a freezing cold shower before a match. He listens to music to help him focus.

Rituals, while interesting, no doubt barely scratch the surface of what these top professionals do to get ready for a match. If you want to play your best tennis, develop your own rituals that power up your body and mind. Watching the Tennis Channel before you play may inspire you. Likewise, relaxing with your favorite music, or visualizing solid play may work for you. Perhaps meditation is your thing. Whatever ritual you establish, it must include the following items:

- Eat right. If you are undernourished prior to a match, you will feel fatigued long before the match is over.

On the other hand, eat too much too close to match time, and you will be sluggish from the outset. It's also important to eat foods you know will agree with your stomach. Now is not the time to experiment.

- Get enough rest the night before you play. If you have a hectic schedule, even a short nap can be beneficial.
- Hydrate! Dehydration will affect your energy and your judgment. Drink enough water before you get to the court, at least 16 ounces two hours before you play. It is much harder than most of us realize to catch up once play begins, especially in hot weather. Remember the day before your match is the most important. Too much water on the day of your match will leave you sluggish.
- Come to the match prepared for the unexpected. Be sure to have a snack, plenty of water, a towel and an extra shirt available.
- Check your equipment. There is no excuse for showing up to a match with a racket that needs to be restrung. Check the condition of your grip too and have a replacement on hand.

Make the Most of Warm-ups

Being a tennis instructor involves a lot of time on the court demonstrating various shots and in turn observing players as they try to master them. Over the years I've learned that some of the most productive time I spend with my students is in conversation about different aspects of their game.

One thing I always ask players is, "What are you doing during warm-ups?"

"Assessing my opponent," is a common answer.

When I say, "Good, what are you looking for?"

Most students will say something like, "I want to know if they can hit a backhand."

That is not a bad answer, but there is a good deal more you should be evaluating during pre-match warm-ups.

- How well does your opponent move?
- When checking their backhand notice how well they handle high and low balls. Do they hit a one-handed or two-handed backhand?
- Does your opponent hit with a lot of top-spin, slice or both?
- Are they comfortable at the net? If they don't ask for some net practice, chances are excellent they don't like to come to the net.
- Does your opponent volley with an open face? If not, you know you can feed them low balls during the match.
- When it's time to practice serves, be sure to notice how much pace, spin and slice they use. If they have spin or slice, you will have to adjust to the ball, moving in a different direction. Observing the quality and characteristics of your opponent's serve, may help you decide whether you want to serve or return to start the match.
- Do they ask for overheads? If not, be sure to lob this player early in the match to see how they react. Like net play, if they don't ask for lobs during warm-up, they probably don't like hitting them.

- Are they lefthanded or right handed? I know this one seems obvious but you would be surprised by how many people overlook this important detail. Not only is it important to know which side of the player to pick on, but if they have spin you will have to adjust to the ball moving from a different direction. Obviously, in a rally where you are on the ad side of the court, chances are, you will be hitting backhands while your opponent is hitting forehands.

Warm-up is also a time to prepare yourself for the match.

- Warm up your shoulder. I like doing windmills at least ten in each direction. You use your shoulder more than you might realize, especially for forehands and the serve. If you don't warm up your shoulder adequately, you might not finish high enough on your follow through resulting in lack of depth and direction.
- Evaluate your stroke's depth. Are you getting the ball past the service line? If not, now is the time to fix it. Check the height of your follow through and make sure your racket is getting below the ball.
- When you volley during warm-up, volley for depth. Aim for the last few feet of the court. Shorter volleys are usually the easy ones, but deep volleys can be more effective.
- Are you hitting your spots on your serve? I recommend you warm up your second serve and slice serve first. When that's done, alternate between first and second serves. This is important for confidence and to get into a rhythm. If you hit 8 out of 10 serves into the net what

are you thinking? Today is not going to be a great serving day. Better to miss your serve long during warm-up, not into the net. This is a physiological trick that was taught to me years ago. It might not sound like a big deal but bringing a serve down is easy. You can adjust your toss so it's more out in front of you or make sure to use your wrist, or possibly just add a little spin.

- Assess which side of the court you're on. Where is the sun? Which way is the wind blowing? Be ready to make adjustments accordingly.
- Here's one last piece of advice about warm-ups. When you spin, presumably to determine who will serve first, spin before you start your warmup. Remember that one of the options is to decide on which side of the court you will begin play. Consider the sun which may require a lower ball toss when you serve. The wind is another factor. If you hit with the wind you'll need to add spin and keep the ball lower. Hitting against the wind requires more pace. Obviously, winning the first game of your match is a good thing. Do what you can at the outset to improve your odds.

Get the Most Out of Practice

How do you get the most out of practice? It's a good question because if you're going to invest the time to improve your game, it would be a shame to waste it. I have seen countless players flailing away at balls popping out of the ball machine to no particular purpose. They would be better off playing in matches which is, of course, a great way to improve your game.

To practice effectively you must start with a desire to achieve a higher level of performance. If you have that, you're much more likely to spend the time it takes to improve all aspects of your game. Without a desire to improve, practice becomes drudgery. Practice with someone who shares your enthusiasm for the game and has a positive attitude. Practicing with someone who has a negative attitude is the worst. You're a tennis player not a cheerleader. Constantly having to pump up your partner can reduce your own effectiveness.

Here are three techniques you can use to maximize practice time:

1. **Have a specific goal**
   What are you working on? Start with your weakest area and devote the time you need to make improvements. Let's say you're working on your serve. Which part of the serve is most troublesome? Whether it's your toss, or your grip, or your point of contact with the ball, focus on that until you get comfortable. Don't hesitate to experiment with different techniques. That's what practice is for. Recognize that changes don't take hold over night. It takes time to build new muscle memory. For your practice to be effective you need to have specific goals in mind.

2. **Repetition**
   Repeatedly hitting the same stroke to the same spot on the court will improve your ability to hit that stroke, but it won't necessarily improve your results. Tennis is a game that requires you to be able to hit the ball to

different areas on the court. If you're working on your backhand for example, you might focus initially on your form and getting the ball over the net and in play.

At this point, your backhand may not have much pace and you may not be able to control the ball's direction. However, once you are confident that you can reliably count on your backhand to do its basic job, you can begin to focus on putting the ball where you want it to go. Consider using targets (Can of balls, ball hopper, cones etc.) to help with accuracy. You can add pace and top spin. You can learn to hit a backhand slice.

Each of these skills takes lots of repetition in practice.

3. **Intensity matters**

When I'm giving lessons I often see players on adjacent courts supposedly practicing. Too often what they are doing is casually hitting the ball to each other instead of going full tilt after every ball that comes their way. If you give less than your best effort in practice, chances are you will play the same way in your next match. When professional tennis players practice they go all out.

4. **Make Mistakes**

Einstein once said, "Anyone who has never made a mistake has never tried anything new." Almost everything I have learned in tennis has come from making a mistake first. When you're in a clinic or practice session, don't be afraid to make mistakes. Many players feel like they are letting others down, or might feel embarrassed, but remember its PRACTICE. You're not supposed to be perfect. Think about your first attempts to hit a forehand. Most of us hit a bunch into the net and some balls went too long. You were making mistakes, lots of them. That was how you learned to hold the racket, develop the necessary footwork and follow through. Even if you never took a lesson, eventually you would learn how to hit a solid groundstroke if you experimented enough. When you're learning something new, expect to make errors. That is the path to success.

When it's time to play a match leave your thoughts about technique on the practice court. Just play your game and stick to your strategy. Play as well as you can and leave the assessment to after the match. If you keep "thinking" the way you do during practice, you'll be putting yourself under unnecessary pressure. Enjoy the game.

During the Match

Movement and Court Coverage

Having great strokes is very important in tennis, but I've known many players who don't. Yet, they have been very successful due to their smart court coverage. There are of course, many different scenarios as different points unfold that require you to move to cover the court. As you read this book you will be exposed to a variety of these situations along with strategies to help you improve your game. In general though, there are some areas you can focus on that will help you shrink the court and end points on your terms.

1. **Track the ball**

   In basketball and soccer for example, players are told to follow the ball. It's no different in tennis. Tracking the ball involves moving side to side and/or moving forward or backward. In doubles, you and your partner follow the shot. Remember, your shot dictates what you do next. Many players will hit a shot, good or bad, and then wait to see what their opponents do in return. If you or your partner hit a good shot for example an offensive shot (deep, well angled, a lot of pace) that puts your opponent on their heels. That's when you close to the net so you can be rewarded for your efforts. If your shot is subpar you still follow it side to side, but you don't get as close to the net. I see too many players who are great at tracking their ball early in a match, only to stop doing it as the match moves along. Take it from me, players who don't track the ball throughout the entire match, aren't going to win many matches.

2. **Know your role on the court**
   When you're at the net you have a very important role: You're the aggressor, doing your best to finish points. The bad news is you usually don't know where your partner is going with his next shot. Yet, you must be able to follow your partner's shot in order to close off the court and give you a chance to finish the point. At the net you must have your head on a swivel watching the opposing net player and then reacting to the player who will be returning the ball.

3. **Overstate the obvious.**
   I feel many experienced players who have played with the same partner for a long period think that their partner knows what they are going to do next and in many cases they do. But I'd rather be safe than sorry. One of the most common scenarios I see is on overheads. The net player gets an overhead and nothing is said (Like "I got it," or "mine.") Then the deeper player runs to back up his partner and, before you know it, both players are on the same side of the court. The other example I see is when the net player gets aggressive and decides to cross

without saying anything (e.g. "switch.") If they don't end the point then, you have the same problem, two players on the same side of the court. With one side of the court wide open, chances are excellent that your opponents are going to win the point on their next shot. Remember the pros communicate. So should you.

Playing Defense

Most of us would rather play offense, ripping a forehand down the line for a winner. It's hard to beat the feeling one gets hitting powerful shots that overwhelm the opposition. Yet, the best pros in the game from Nadal to Radwanska know how and when to play defense. If you want to improve the quality of your game, you must learn to play defense.

Defense comes into play in two situations. When your opponent hits an exceptional shot; a ball that sends you into the alley, a lob over your head, an exceptionally deep shot or even a well placed first serve. Naturally, the other scenario would be *you* hit a poor shot, a short lob, a floater, or a weak second serve. Certainly there are a good number of situations where you will suddenly find yourself in a defensive situation. Let's discuss the most common situations and how you should handle them.

Your opponent hits a great shot

First serve

Your opponent's first serve is so good that your only option is to block it, which often results in a shorter reply than you would like. Now you're on defense. Be prepared to shorten your swing, possibly several times, if your opponent continues to attack aggressively. Like a boxer who finds it necessary to block punches coming his way until he sees an opening, you should be ready to defend your side of the court and look for your chance to go on offense.

Crosscourt rollover

If your opponent hits a good crosscourt rollover, taking you out wide, you have two options. If you're pulled out so far that you are standing in the doubles alley, hit the ball crosscourt about six feet over the net. The extra height you put on the ball will give you a bit more time to recover. In fact, a looper (See Shot Making section) is also a good shot to hit in this situation. What if you're pulled completely outside the court? My friend, it's time to pull the trigger! Try to end the point by aggressively going down the line. Look at it this way: in this situation, one way or the other the point is likely to be over.

High backhand

Your adversary hits a high ball to your backhand. This is a difficult shot, even for many touring pros. If you hit a two-handed backhand, one way to handle it is to swing very hard, shoulder high, cross court. As an alternative, you can hit a backhand lob. Even though I teach 40 hours a week and play at least once a week, I might hit four two-handed, backhand lobs a year.

Now, if you have a one-handed backhand, your best option is to lob. In fact, many players who normally use a two-handed backhand will switch to one hand to hit a backhand lob. The other thing a one hander can do is hit a slice, a shot that has served Roger Federer well in this situation for years. The point here is to know which shot is your strength and don't second guess your options.

Lob over your head

Lobbing the ball back to your opponent is always an option in this situation, but you can also wait until the ball bounces and hit a crosscourt shot. One thing you should avoid: focusing on your opponent instead of the ball. This is no time to get lazy! You want to overrun the ball so you can get behind it, in the best position to hit your shot. You don't want to be even with the ball when it bounces. Otherwise, you'll be forced to hit a racket ball like shot, or even worse, the blind shovel lob from your chest over your head.

Drop shot

I know: It's tempting to just give your opponent the point and a dirty look rather than run. But run you must. The easiest thing to do with a drop shot is to drop shot back. Keep the ball low to the net. This shot requires touch. If you hit a pop-up, you're probably toast. The more advanced play would be to hit the ball behind your opponent's feet. Most players are several steps inside the baseline already when they hit a drop shot, and they may be moving up more expecting a drop shot in return.

You hit a poor shot

You hit a short lob

Let's face it, even at the baseline you're a sitting duck. There is only one thing you can do. Hesitate momentarily and then guess what your opponent will do and move to the left or right accordingly. This sounds obvious, but time and again I've seen players stand still in this situation and watch the ball go by them. Now, suppose you guess right, now what? Your best options are to return with a slice lob or, treat it like a volley and block the ball back. Which of these shots you will hit depends on what your opponent does after she hits the ball. If she moves forward, hit the slice lob. If she stands pat, block the ball back to her. These options will become easier to decipher as you begin to understand your opponent's tendencies.

You hit a floater that lands near the service line

In this scenario where you hit the ball, matters. If you hit it wide, your opponent is more likely to hit a crosscourt return. Your job is to move toward the alley, where the ball will most likely be. If you hit it down the middle, again, hesitate momentarily and then guess what your opponent will do and move to the left or right accordingly. Keep in mind that unlike the weak lob you hit, your opponent doesn't have as much time to make a decision about where to hit the ball or be deceptive about his intentions.

You hit a weak second serve

Your placement of the serve determines what you will do. Usually, when you hit this serve you're inside the baseline at its conclusion. The first thing to do is go back behind the baseline. If you don't do this, chances are you're going to be trying to hit a half-volley on your next shot. While it's doable, your odds are considerably better hitting from behind the baseline.

You attempt a passing shot

The pace you put on the ball dictates your action. If you hit the ball with pace, move to the open court because that's where your opponent's volley is mostly likely to go. It's a higher percentage shot. You have to move to the area where the ball is likely to go. If you hit it with little pace, stay put! Why? With a slower ball they have more time to decide where to hit their return. If you move, they just might hit the ball behind you.

Look For Tendencies

Do you have playing partners and opponents you play on a regular basis? A lot of recreational players do. What are your opponents most comfortable doing? We all have tendencies in our game. If you take the time to notice your opponent's tendencies, you can make it harder for them to hit their go-to shots. Taking the time to notice adversaries' tendencies will make you more competitive the next time you play them. What do they like to do? How can you combat their play and incorporate it into your game?

For example, you can frustrate a player who loves to hit the inside out forehand by moving to the ad side of the court to get ready for what's coming. What can he do? Hit the shot anyway or, instead, go for the much harder inside in forehand down the line.

Then there's the opponent who loves to hit slice shots. Give her more top spin to make it harder to hit that shot.

Knowing tendencies is especially valuable when you're on defense. Have you ever noticed that many players prefer to hit their overheads crosscourt? If you hit a poor lob, you can hesitate and then break for his crosscourt return. Your odds of guessing right in that situation are greatly improved. And, when your opponent eventually decides he has to hit to the other side, he may be uncomfortable doing it.

Notice too whether your opponent feeds off pace as many players do. Throw in some changeups to expose poor footwork. See if they can generate their own pace.

My point about all this is simple. Identify and take advantage of people's tendencies. It will allow you to play better defense.

Be Aggressive

Many players say, "Today is the day I'm going to be aggressive." Then, after two miscues their thought process changes to, "this isn't working…maybe next match." Obviously, being aggressive is an important tactic in both singles and doubles. One of my biggest challenges with adults is to get them to take chances. Remember that you're not going to win every point, but playing not to lose doesn't lead to winning very often. Let's take a look at four opportunities to be aggressive in doubles at the net where being aggressive is a must.

1. **Body shots at the baseline**
   When your partner hits a shot at the body of your opponent who is on the baseline, be ready to close. This is a great play since your opponent is jammed which usually results in a weak shot with no angles. Players frequently fail to recognize this opportunity, missing a scoring chance.

2. **Look for balls in the alley**
   You've probably been told to track the ball in doubles but that isn't always the best strategy. That's the case most of the time, but not always. When you are at the net and your partner is at the baseline look for balls that land in the alley of your opponent's crosscourt. Hesitate slightly and move to the middle when the ball lands in the alley. Your partner has hit a great shot! For your opponent to change the direction of the ball and go down the line will take tour level skill. You will be amazed how many times you have an opportunity to end the point. Of course, if the ball lands in the singles court, cover your alley.

3. **Watch for low balls**
   You're at the net and your partner is back. When you opponent retrieves a low ball their only goal is to get it over the net. Squeeze the middle and win more points. If they happen to get the ball over your head, or by you, your partner will still have an opportunity to make a play.

4. **The middle of the court**
   You're at the net and your partner hits a ball that flirts with the net person, but stays in the middle without the net person hitting it. Go to the middle of the court. Remember angles create angles, but this is the opposite situation. Balls in the middle tend to stay in the middle. Now and then you might get burned down the alley, but the plusses outweigh the minuses.

When you are being aggressive, move at an angle. Closing at an angle is a must because if you don't, your contact point probably won't be from an offensive position. The other key factor in closing correctly is that if you do it well, you should get the ball higher above the net and closer, which will result in a better angle. Then you will be able to hit down on the ball or shorten your opponent's reaction time.

When are you being too aggressive? How do you know when you're overdoing it?

1. **Contact Point**
   Are you making contact with the ball out in front or at your side? It must be out in front so you can either create an angle or hit down on the ball. If you wait too long to hit the ball it becomes much harder to keep your eye on it. Why?

2. **The "big step"**
   Are you taking too big of a step? If so you better end the point because your recovery will take longer than normal. You really don't want to lunge to make a shot. Remember good posture is important and so are small steps for balance.

3. **Are you changing the direction of the ball at the wrong time?**
   It's well documented that when you change the direction of the ball from crosscourt to down the line your unforced errors increase. Why? The net is higher; the court is shorter. Even the amount of court you have to cover increases. This is not to say it can't be done, but you must wait for a controllable ball. A controllable ball is one that has less pace; a ball you can move

> forward into the court to hit. This sounds simple, but sometimes it's hard to think this way when the court looks wide open. Stick with this principle and you will be amazed by your results.

By taking some calculated risks, you will win more and soon you'll be playing at a higher level.

Handling the Tie Breaker

It's a tight match. It comes down to a tie breaker to decide the set or even the match. That's when players suddenly change their strategy as if a tie breaker changes the size of the court or the shape of the ball. They alter their style of play, often to their detriment. As I said earlier, when you play not to lose rather than playing to win, the results are often disappointing.

If you've gotten into a tie breaker, things have been going pretty well for you. Never mind that you thought you should have won easily. There is nothing you can do about what happened up to this point. This is not the time to hit the panic button. Just because you're in a tie breaker is no reason to radically change what you were doing during the match.

Here are four things to keep in mind when you begin a tie breaker:

1. If you dread tie breakers, guess what? You'll probably lose a lot more of them than you should. Instead of dreading the moment, recognize it for what it is: FUN. You get to play a little longer, doing what you love doing.
2. Your first serve percentage in a tie breaker has to be high, above 60%. First serves are crucial in a tie breaker

and not because your opponent might crush a return. It's for your own psychological well being. Let's face it. In a tie breaker, miss your first serve, you immediately get tense, fearing the dreaded double fault, a real no-no in a tie breaker. Keep it simple. Serve to the body. A body serve forces your opponent to move. It's a higher percentage shot because a slight miss right or left will still be in. If his feet get stuck you can get some easy points. And don't be afraid to put some spin on your first serve, something I hope you do regularly in every match.

3. Go for higher percentage shots, but don't slow down your swing. If your opponent is feeling a bit nervous, chances are his footwork will suffer. Do what you do best. If you love charging the net, don't suddenly become a baseline player. Employ the strategies that got you into the tie breaker in the first place.
4. Practice tie breakers. That's right; you can improve your performance in tie break situations with practice. You and your practice partner should include tie breakers in your regular practice routine. One of the key ingredients to winning a tie breaker is the ability to stay focused for 7 to 10 points without a break. Knowing the rules for a tie breaker is another advantage. Let your opponent worry about where to serve from and when you switch sides.

Relax and Have Fun

I love watching sports. The best athletes make it look easy. Why? They are, of course, exceptional athletes. They have practiced their skills thousands of times. However, I think a key reason they consistently perform well under pressure is they can relax in any situation. A baseball player like the New York Yankee's, Derek Jeter never looked like he was trying hard. The New England Patriots quarterback, Tom Brady, seems to hit his receivers effortlessly.

In most sports, there is an expression called the "whip effect." The more relaxed you are the faster you are able to execute, whether it's swinging a bat, throwing a ball, or swinging a tennis racket. In tennis the only way to achieve this is with light, relaxed grip pressure.

As a tennis player, you've no doubt experienced moments when you were in the zone, where everything you did seemed to work. If you stop and think about it, in those moments were you tense or relaxed? Confident or doubtful? Were you worried about whether you won the last point in those moments or were you caught up in the sheer excitement and joy of competing? I'll wager you were relaxed, confident and experiencing the thrill of playing the game.

Think about the best return you ever hit. I bet it was on a serve that was out. Why does this happen? It happens because there were no consequences. I wish I could say just go out and play and don't worry about the outcome. Not many tennis players are built that way. But what you can do is learn relaxation techniques you can use between points. Here are a few you might want to try.

- Hold your racket in your non-dominant hand or put it under your arm after points. It is very important to have as little tension in your dominant arm possible.

- Go for a walk to get the third ball. Taking time between points is crucial so that you can regroup.
- Straighten your strings like the pros. In this day and age you might not have to straighten your strings as much because of polyester strings, but it does give you a moment to focus before the next point.
- Be sure to sit down on changeovers whether or not you need a rest. Sitting down relaxes you. Give yourself a moment to review your strategy.
- Breathe. This sounds obvious, but before every point, especially when I serve, I take a deep breath before starting the point. Again, the lower the tension in your body, the more you'll benefit from the whip effect.

You can reduce stress *during* a point too.

- Grunting or breathing during the point is also a must. When I was growing up, my mother used to play tennis and she was always in great shape. But, she would hold her breath on every shot and if she had a rally longer than 3 shots she was ready to collapse. I find that many players lose their grunt when the match gets tight, when it should be constant the whole match. However, don't become one of those over the top grunters that can be heard from the club house. If it's natural, fine. If it's merely imitating your favorite pro, lose it.
- Use ball height, or spin to slow things down during the point.

Playing Surface

One of the raging debates in the world of tennis today is why Americans aren't dominating the sport the way they once did. Some say it's the way they're taught. Others say American players today lack drive. Still others blame the hard court surface Americans play on most frequently. I'm convinced it's the latter.

European tennis players grow up playing on clay, a huge advantage. Clay courts are slower, making points last longer. This teaches players to have patience in setting up points. They learn to massage a point to their advantage. It's not easy to blow an opponent off the court in two or three shots. A clay surface forces players to create more angles, use more spin and focus more on placement.

If you can, practice and play on a clay surface, including Har-Tru courts. It will give you the best opportunity to play longer points and learn to appreciate the value and effectiveness of putting spin on the ball. On a clay surface, when you put topspin on the ball, it kicks higher than on a hard surface. Slice the ball and watch it die after it bounces.

You will find that if you practice on clay, what you learn there will translate well to a hard court surface. Even though the pace of play on hard courts is faster, the time spent developing angles, top spin and slice will serve you well. Obviously you can practice these maneuvers on hard surface courts too, but you probably won't get to hit as many balls. If you don't have access to a clay court, try practicing using only half the court to improve your ability to hit angles and improve ball placement.

I'm Having a Bad Day. What Now?

It happens to all of us. We step onto the court well prepared and confident. Yet, nothing seems to work. Serves are wide; ground strokes go long, or into the net. Don't even ask about volleys or backhands. When you're having a bad day there are some things you can do to correct the problem, or at least minimize the damage.

- Play conservatively, hitting high percentage shots. Forget the alleys and hit your second serve on your first.
- Add topspin and slice to your shots. Spin equals control.
- Slow everything down. **If your usual swing number is 7 back it down to six.**
- Search for the issue that is causing you the most trouble. For example, if your ground strokes aren't working, examine your footwork, make sure you're getting your racket back early and your eyes are focused on the ball.
- Keep moving. For example, when the third ball is on your half of the court, jog to where it is and pick it up.
- This is not the time to think about technique. Remember that it's highly unlikely that you can change your technique successfully during a match. Instead, be very specific about where you want the ball to go. I'm frequently amazed when I have players do a drill where I place cones for them and say, "try to hit them." They quickly become adept at hitting the spot they're aiming for. They're now focused on a specific target rather than technique.

The Three Strikes Rule

You're playing at the net. Your partner serves and the returner hits a beauty down the line, passing you. What do you do, guard the line for the rest of the match? That strategy will protect you from the down the line shot of course, but you've also taken away the threat of being aggressive when the ball is near the middle. What should you do?

Recognize that one passing shot, one perfectly placed lob or a single dramatic crosscourt rollover doesn't mean your opponent has that shot in their arsenal. Too often players overreact when they see a shot like this. Make your opponent hit that shot three times in the match to prove she really has it. One time, even twice could be she was lucky. Three times says it's more than likely you have to defend yourself against that shot.

Let's not forget the flipside to the three strike rule. When you try a shot and miss three times, go to plan B. It's just not your day for that shot.

Seven Strategies for a Windy Day

What is the answer when the ball is blowing in the wind? It can be a very frustrating experience to play a match on a windy day. The wind makes the ball do funny things. Yet, there are times when you have to play on windy days. You can curse your bad luck, or make the most of it. Here are seven strategies to help you enjoy the game on windblown days:

1. Lower your expectations. No one has ever come off the court on a windy day and said, "That was the best match I ever played."

2. Wind has a tendency to expose poor footwork. You have to move to the ball and be ready to adjust quickly.
3. Focus on hitting the ball to the center of the court. Angles can be costly if the ball moves more than expected.
4. Lower the toss on your serve.
5. When hitting into the wind use a long, full stroke.
6. When hitting with the wind, employ lots of spin and keep the ball close to the net.
7. Get to the net more often. Lobbing is an unlikely strategy. More net play will help take the guess work out of your groundstrokes.

Seven things you should discuss with your doubles partner

One of the things I notice when I watch doubles matches is the lack of communication between partners. Yet, good communication can greatly improve your chances of winning more points and more matches. Here are seven points you and your partner should be talking about throughout the course of a match.

1. **Who serves first?**

   Many players assume that the partner with the bigger serve should serve first. The question you and your partner should ask is, which one of you holds serve more often? After you've played together for a while, you should know the answer to that question. Another factor you should consider is which one of you gets off to a faster start in matches? If you take a few games to really get going, and your partner doesn't need much warmup, let her serve first.

2. **Where you will serve**
   If your partner knows your intentions when you serve, then he has a good idea of which way to move once the ball passes him on its way to the receiver. When serving to the T from the deuce side of the court, for example, it allows your partner to take two to three steps toward the center of the court to squeeze the middle. After all, the player returning serve is more likely to hit a defensive shot down the middle with a bit of angle. This creates an excellent opportunity for the net player to be aggressive, especially when the server gives him a heads-up. When serving out wide on the deuce side, your partner will have to cover the line and react to the crosscourt.

3. **Where you plan to hit your return of serve**
   Talking about where to serve is more common, but talking about where you might return is not discussed often enough. Keep your conversation brief though. Be mindful of the rule stipulating that you play at the server's pace. Tell your partner where you plan to hit your service return so she can move to close off the court, or realize the next ball may be coming in her direction. By the way, if you plan to hit a lob on your return of serve, reserve this shot mainly for second serves when you are in a position to hit a forehand.

The lob is a touch shot. Trying to hit one off of a first serve, which often has more pace than a second serve, can be difficult. It requires a very delicate balance to be able to take pace off the ball and have it land where you want it to go. When you tell your partner you plan to lob on the return, it gives her the time to prepare for several outcomes. If, for example, your lob return is weak, your partner could be a sitting duck for an overhead smash return. On the other hand, assuming the ball lands where you want it to, your opponent may well send a lob back your way in response. You want your partner to be in a good position to take advantage of that whenever possible. Likewise, if you plan to hit your return down the line, your partner can expect a volley coming her way if you don't pass the net person. Let your partner know your intentions.

4. **Discuss whether to poach**
   If you and your partner are skilled net players, poaching makes perfect sense. When should you poach? If your partner can place the serve well and control their spin, your opponent's returns will tend to be weaker, which gives you an ideal opportunity to poach. If your partner is adept at serving to the T or the body, those are other opportunities to poach. One strategy I highly recommend is to poach on the first point of every match when your team is serving. Why? Think about it. How many players are really comfortable hitting the ball down the line on their first return of serve of the match? When you poach so soon in a match it sends a

message: "We know how to play doubles." It can also set up your opponent for a fake poach at any time during the match.

What about hand signals? Some players don't care for them, but they are useful. Keep in mind that hand signals save time, which is helpful, especially when things are going well for your team and you don't want to lose your momentum. One of my students gave me what I thought was a memorable and effective hand signaling technique based on the well known game of rock, paper, scissors. The rock, or fist, means you will not poach on the next point. Like a rock, you'll stay put. Paper, the open hand, says you're going, floating to the other side. And scissors, two fingers indicates you will fake a poach by taking a step and returning to your position. There are several different methods you can use, but it's very important that you communicate your intentions with your partner. As with the Australian formation, if you are not at least occasionally poaching, you are limiting your chances of success. Being predictable is a boon to your opponents.

Poaching, or going Australian, is recommended mainly for the first serve but you must do it occasionally on the second serve. Otherwise no pressure is being applied. Preplan a couple a points ahead when poaching. Obviously if you meet and poach on the very next point every time, your opponents will soon be on high alert whenever you meet. When you meet say, "After we win this point, we'll poach the next time the first serve goes in." Variety is what makes the good, great.

5. The Australian formation

If your serve has been broken twice, or you're playing a fantastic returner, you and your partner should consider using the Australian formation when you serve. With this formation you are trying to induce the returner to hit the ball down the line. That wide open space they see can be irresistible. Yet, for the down the line shot to work, they have to successfully change the direction of the ball, hit it over the highest part of net with less court space at their disposal. Remember, a cross court return in doubles gives players an extra 8 feet of court, and the net is 6 inches lower. Note too that as the server in this formation you are responsible for covering the other side of the court should your opponent hit a successful down the line return. In addition, with the Australian formation, the net player will occasionally cross over to the other side to keep the returner honest. If you are not switching to an Australian formation when your serve is broken a couple of times, you are limiting yourself as a doubles player.

Understandably, many players fight this formation until they grasp the mechanics and the strategy. With the Australian formation, the net player starts on the same side as the server lined up slightly to the outside of him. This will allow a better view of the "T" and the server is less likely to hit her partner. Remember when the serve lands in, the net player will mostly stay in her position. She doesn't move because the opposing net player will block your alley and this will allow the net player to take the middle and then some.

When you try Australian, if you aren't having success, examine placement of your serve. In this formation serves need to go to the T. Also, when crossing, be sure to make your move as the returner pulls her racket back. In this scenario its better for the net player to go a little bit early. Move at an angle toward the net. By going earlier your opponents may see what your plan is, but if you can get your opponent to change her mind, usually their return suffers. In any case you want to make sure the court is covered. Try to hit your volley at or to the inside of the opposing net player. Going back crosscourt is doable but you must be well versed in taking the pace off the ball to land it short and at an angle.

Using the "I" formation also works but it requires the net person to crouch down and have a foot in both service boxes. This is also a great play, but for me crouching down has its issues as I get older and have to get up quickly from a much lower position.

Many players don't see these formations very often and really don't know how to beat them. Frequently I get asked "what do you do when someone goes Australian?" My answer is before the serve is hit know where you are going to return the ball and don't react to the net person. It's a guessing game and that's one of the reasons it's so effective.

6. Coaching your partner during a match

By all means, discuss what's working for your team as well as any weaknesses you observe on the opposing side of the court. The trick is to do so without coaching each other. Players rarely appreciate coaching from a player at the same level. When discussing your partner's play, compliment rather than coach. This is the best way to avoid upsetting your partner or creating misunderstandings that can cost you the match. When I'm teaching, I often say "You're only as good as your partner". This statement is meant to be funny but there is a lot of truth to it. Make sure your partner's confidence is all that it can be.

Remember that what you say can stick with someone the entire match. Don't criticize shot selection or encourage low percentage plays like drop shots from behind the baseline or down the line returns.

7. **Who should play which side of the court?**
Obviously, you and your partner will make this decision prior to playing the match. If one of you is a righty and the other a lefty, usually the right handed player plays the add side, while the left-handed player is on the deuce side of the court. That way, you're both hitting forehands when the ball is in the middle of the court. It's not foolproof, but it's a good starting point.

In the majority of situations, you both hit right-handed. Usually, one of you will tend to be a more aggressive player than the other. If that's the case the more aggressive player takes the add side of the court. This works well because their forehand is in the middle and it allows them the opportunity to be a "ball hog". Let me assure you being a ball hog is not a bad thing. You have to want the ball. Wanting the ball is a great thing as long as you're not so aggressive that you are taking high risk shots.

How do you know if you're being too aggressive? If you are unable to keep the ball in front of you, you are being a "ball hog". If you are not able to move at an angle (meaning you're going straight across). You're being a "ball hog". Remember if both feet cross the dividing line between the service boxes your partner must now switch. I have two points of no return in tennis. One being the aforementioned and the second being if you are coming from the baseline and you cross the service line you are now playing the net whether you like it or not, unless you are an Olympic sprinter and can get back to the baseline.

Stop Socializing on the Court

Listen: If you want to socialize with your opponent or your doubles partner while you're playing your match, go right ahead. Be prepared, however to lose some points in the process. I have seen this scenario played out many times. Recreational players are out to enjoy themselves. They talk about their work, their kids, the fabulous vacation they took to Bali, or the latest Cabernet they tried.

Enjoyable topics, but unless you are skilled at consciously cutting off any residual thoughts you may be in trouble. It's nearly impossible to focus when your mind is on something you want to add to the conversation at the next break, daydreaming about your own vacation plans, or wondering what your opponent meant by his last comment. The mind cannot hold two thoughts simultaneously. So when you should be thinking about where you are going to return the next serve, instead you're making a mental note to get that chicken Kiev recipe. Not properly focused, you return the serve wide and its 15-love.

My advice is this. If you really want to improve your game you must save the chatter and social networking for before and after the match. Once the match starts, do your best to limit idle talk. Keep in mind that your opponent may well be aware of the benefits of distracting you.

I realize that you may be thinking, "Socializing is one of the reasons I love playing tennis. The banter is too much fun to give up." I can understand that. If that describes you, let me make a suggestion. Come up with a ritual that helps you refocus before you start the next point.

When to Play Back in Doubles

There are not many scenarios where I like to see both players playing back at the baseline. For one thing, it's too passive. I'm addressing it though, because I know it happens. Play back if your opponent's first serve is overwhelming you and his partner is having a field day with your weak returns, maybe even hitting you. For one thing it gives you more reaction time. If the server misses his first serve, your partner returns to the forward position. Before moving all the way to the baseline you might even try starting a couple of feet behind the service line. Yes, this is "no-man's land," but it will give you a little more time to react and it allows you to get back to the net more easily than from behind the baseline.

Another time to try this is when nothing is working for you, especially if your opponents don't have much touch at the net.

Try not to make a habit of the "back" formation though. It's much easier to close out points from the net. I'll let you in on a little secret. When I see both players move back it's kind of like waving the white flag. I start to smile because they're probably out of ideas and very often, the end is near. You may have noticed that both players back is done more often at the pro level. They do this because the speed of the ball at that level is much greater.

Finishing a Point

We've all been there. You set up a point beautifully, only to dump what should have been a winner into the net. Or, you're up in games 5-2 and before you know it, it's 5-4 and your opponent has the momentum.

Why is it that the floater at the net, the one you can't wait to put away for an easy point causes so much trouble? One reason shots like this can be harder to make than they should be is we tend to get lazy. We forget we still have to move our feet to get in the best position to hit the ball.

Sometimes you hit a deep smash that looks like a winner, but much to your surprise it come right back. You thought the point was over and you relaxed instead of remaining in the ready position. A lot of players who do remain alert just try to hit the ball harder, often with disastrous results. As we discussed elsewhere, a better strategy in this situation is to take some pace off the ball and create an angle, or, keep them running. When I'm playing, at no point in a match do I say the next shot is a winner. Winners just happen. If you keep your opponent running, the court will open up and you might even tire them out for the next few points.

Finishing a point actually begins by having a strategy when the point starts. A strategy puts you in a position at the outset to win the point. Get your hands back into the ready position until the point is won. Just remember not to let your guard down. Things to look for: When you miss an easy shot are your feet side by side or did you take one giant step? If so, you were reaching and were probably off balance.

Remember, in tennis, you must take many small steps to get into the perfect position. Do you hear squeaking or shuffling of your shoes? That's music to a tennis pro's ears. Did you keep the ball out in front of you when trying to finish the point? Many times players reach to the side to finish the point when they should be moving forward at an angle keeping the ball out in front of them. How far did your hands go behind you? How far you take your hands back depends on the height and speed of the incoming ball. The point is, if you are consistently hitting long when trying to finish a point your hands are going too far back. Ending the point, or hitting a winner is not always done in a spectacular manner. Winning a point is not always gratifying, but winning a match should be.

Closing out the Match

For years players have had problems closing out a match when they're in a great position to win it. This is not an uncommon situation. Too often, players get nervous when they have the lead. They're afraid if they lose, someone will say they choked. Sometimes I think it happens when a player is about to beat someone he wasn't expected to beat. "I'm about to win! Can this really be happening?" That's when self doubt can begin to creep in.

Rather than worrying about losing, embrace the moment and go for it. I'm not suggesting you throw caution to the wind and take unnecessary chances. Play the way you would if you were even at two games each. When you have the lead you have nothing to complain about. Who cares if they get a few points or win a game?

When you have the lead, stay aggressive, hit with pace and stay active at the net. One thing you don't do is play not to lose. That's when you're more likely to get tentative which usually is not how you took the lead to begin with. Instead, take full swings just as you did when the match started. Continue to serve big, but forget aces and go for the body. If you're playing doubles, add more poaching and consider the "I" or Australian formation. The great thing about poaching or going "I" or Australian is you have a responsibility and you won't lose focus. Your partner is depending on you covering a certain part of the court.

It may sound silly but don't forget to breathe! Many adults hate to grunt, but it's very important to exhale as you hit your shot. If someone is grunting or breathing in the beginning of the match and now they're silent, it's rarely a good sign.

Body language is also crucial to closing out you're match. Standing tall, looking confident, says, "I'm going to end this match." It's important for you, but it also lets your opponent know that you're not about to crumble. Positive body language sends a message to your opponent between points *and* when you strike the ball. An example of this would be if someone is not extending their arm at contact and maintaining racket head speed on an overhead or a serve, they are telling their opponent "maybe I can't do this." Extending your arm on your shots shows you're confident and are still in an aggressive mode.

By all means, recognize that having the lead is always a good thing. Like so many things in tennis, experience, especially the experience of winning, builds confidence. It might start with winning a game when you were down love-40. Or, you come from behind to win a set. Ultimately, confidence helps you to close out matches, especially the ones where you took the lead early and held it.

Strategy

Want to Win More Often? Play More Matches

How much tennis have you played in say the last six months? I'm not talking about clinics, ball machine sessions, or hitting ball after ball out of your hopper on a deserted court. While these activities are all valuable, what I really want to know is how many matches have you played? How many times have you tested yourself in actual competition?

Success in tennis is only measured by one yardstick: match play. If you aren't competing, winning some, losing some, always giving every point your best effort, you will soon discover that your game isn't improving the way you hoped it would. Tennis is a very competitive sport. Points, games and matches are won and lost by preparation. Yes, technique, a big serve, solid groundstrokes and the ability to get to the net and volley are critical to your success. But there is a tremendous difference between practicing these things and producing them in the heat of battle. Solid preparation includes playing matches.

What's the difference between practice and match play? Stress. There is nothing stressful about hitting serves for 20 minutes, or striking crosscourt forehands for forty minutes. On the other hand, match play is stressful. In every match, there are only two possible outcomes, winning and losing. And both can be stressful.

My point is there is no way to practice handling stress other than playing matches. Perhaps some of you play tournaments, while others prefer pickup games, or recreational tennis. If you prefer the latter, you can still turn these games into a real match. Play for a can of balls, for instance. Play to see who buys lunch. The stakes don't have to be high, but when the games count, you'll quickly discover what pressure feels like. You will learn to make it work for you too.

Will competitive play make a difference? Let me put it this way. I would bet on the player who competes regularly over the one that doesn't compete. Let me assure you that the latest racket and the hottest strings won't be enough against the player who's competition tough. If you really want to improve your game, play matches that matter. Finally, give yourself an annual goal. For example commit to playing 50 matches this year. I promise, you'll win more matches.

Have a Game Plan

Do you have a progression that you go through when playing a match? What do you do when you have not played someone before and during warm up you see no major flaws? When I ask my students that question, most of them don't really have an answer. By far, most players' game plan is limited to "pick on the backhand." That's not a bad strategy, but what happens when your game improves and you find yourself playing against people who have a solid backhand? Picking on your opponents backhand alone simply won't work.

While you have many options, here's a starting point for your consideration.

Use a looper to the backhand

A looper to the backhand that gets the ball out of the strike zone is a very effective shot. First let me define a looper. A looper is in between a ground stroke and a lob and is most effective with some topspin. This shot is best executed when done crosscourt, not forced down the line. Most players struggle with a higher backhand. This is a great play for you since they will not be able to put much pace on the returning ball when they have to hit it out of their strike zone. If this shot is executed well, players will not have time to back up. They'll be forced to hit the ball shoulder high, or on the rise right after the ball lands in the court.

If you force your opponent to do this, you know that the next ball you will receive will not have much pace on it. That's when you move to the net. Three notes of caution however: If you are playing a "lobber" you may be instigating a lob rally. If your opponent is a lobber, you never want to lob him or her. Lobbers are especially skilled at keeping the ball on the court and taking full advantage of lob placement strategies. Also, be sure not to change the direction of the ball unless it's a controllable ball, i.e. one with less pace or lack of depth.

On the other hand, if you are playing someone who is skilled at taking balls on the rise you may be in for a long day.

In that case, you might need to go to the next strategy in your progression.

Hit at your opponent from the baseline

Most of us know that when you are at the net, your job is to pick on the other net player as long as the ball is above the net. This is not what I'm referring to. When you're hitting baseline to baseline, hit directly at the other baseline player. I know what you're thinking. This sounds like a terrible idea because you're not making your opponent run.

Yet, by hitting directly at the baseline player, you are jamming them up, hindering their direction and taking away their angles. Raphael Nadal thrives on angles. His opponents often try to hit straight at him to minimize Nadal's strength. If executed well during doubles, your partner at the net will look like a hero, or you will get a ball returned short and into your attack zone. This strategy is effective in singles as well as doubles.

I'm a big fan of this strategy early in a match because it's very high percentage and it gives you a target. Many players try hitting away from their opponents early in a rally. The problem with this is that, especially in doubles, there's not much room do this and the chances that you will make an unforced error are high. Another benefit of this tactic is that your opponents may find it hard to figure out what you are doing to them. Unlike lobbing or angling, this strategy is not as obvious. I find many players blaming themselves for poor play, not understanding that this is their opponent's subtle tactic.

Hit to your opponents strength

Hitting to your opponent's strength sets up their weakness. This strategy can be used many different ways, but most people will use this for the backhand. Most players will go to great lengths to guard their weakness.

Many players will stand farther to one side so that it limits the area you have available to hit the ball to their weaker side. If this is the case you must hit it to their stronger side to move them over so that there is now enough court to get the ball to their weakness. A major problem I see is players trying to squeeze a ball into a small portion of the court to pick on a weak shot. The problem with this is you're going to make too many unforced errors in the process.

Use some touch to set up the low backhand

I can assure you that very few players can do much with a low backhand. When you get a controllable ball or maybe a second serve try taking the pace off the ball to force your opponent to run in hitting a low ball. This tactic works best with slice but it's not a must. It's even more effective if they are uncomfortable hitting a one-handed backhand.

Remember that this is not a drop shot. You're not going for a winner. Allow the ball to come to your racket. Your goal here is to make your opponent run and control a low ball, which as we know is a tough play. A great place to aim for with this shot is the corner of the service box.

Now what happens when you execute this shot? Many times the player will not get the ball over the net but if they do it won't have much pace on it much like a drop shot. Recognize this and move forward. If they are lucky enough to get it up as a lob don't worry because it probably won't have much depth, allowing you to respond with an overhead. Even if it does get over your head, you should have plenty of time to run it down because of the high trajectory.

Use shots with varying pace

Have you ever played a match and lost only to come off the court saying "I never got into a rhythm today?" I think most players have and there's a reason. If you use the same pace for the entire match most players will get "grooved" on your strokes. It's like practicing on a ball machine. You get your swing speed down and your footwork does not have to change very much.

Changing the pace of your shots can be very frustrating for your opponent. You can do this by increasing or decreasing your racket head speed or by using multiple spins such as topspin and slice. When you do this well, you will expose poor footwork.

Varying the height of balls can also be very effective as many players are strike zone hitters. Again you can do this by changing your racket head speed and the degree to which you drop your racket under the ball.

You would be amazed at how many high level players, kids and adults, complain about lack of pace. This to me is the worst excuse for a poor performance since a skilled player should be able to dictate the point when an opponent's ball lacks pace. Experiment during a match to see how an adversary adapts and I think you'll be very surprised by your success. Many touring pros such as Fabrice Santoro, aka "The Magician," have made a living by implementing this strategy.

I'm not suggesting that you must use all five strategies during every match. Who you play, the pace of the incoming ball and where the ball lands will dictate your approach in each match. As you gain match experience, selecting the right option will come naturally to you. There are of course, more options than the ones listed here. However, realize that if you've selected a strategy and it isn't working and you're down three games, it's time to move on to another plan.

Play a Game Within a Game

Many times during a match I have to play mental tricks on myself. For example, I tell myself not to hit any more balls into the net. Or I turn to my partner and say lunch is on the person that hits the most balls into the net. Focus on something as simple as this and you will cut down on your unforced errors. By focusing on not making a specific error, you'll be amazed at your consistency and your head will stay in the game.

Another game to play is PING. Many tennis players have played ping pong. Even though determining who serves by PING is not the correct way to do it, this is what most people are accustomed to. Here's how PING works. I make myself say in my head "P" when I hit the first ball of a rally then on the second I say "I" and so on until I get to "G". Most times I don't get to "G" because my opponent has made an error.

While not actually a game, poaching or going Australian is another great way to maintain focus. When I have a lead I like to stay slightly more aggressive. Being slightly more aggressive does not mean swinging out of your Nikes or going for crazy shots, I simply mean be more active at the net. If you poach or go Australian, you have a plan. You and your partner have responsibilities and you can't lose focus because you know you have a certain part of the court to cover.

Managing "No Man's Land"

You're in a rally. Suddenly you find yourself in no man's land! Now what? Every tennis professional in the world recommends that you stay out of "No Man's Land." I'm no different, I suppose but there are exceptions. There are times when you have to be able to play a transition shot from no man's land. Why? Most adults I teach get fixated on getting to the spot where they can hit their first volley. In a perfect world that's great, but it won't always work that way, especially as we get older. Also if you serve and land in the court, many times a good deep return will force you to hit a half volley no matter how quick you might be.

Unless you've been blessed with the quickness of an Olympic sprinter, it can be hard to get from the baseline to the middle of the service box in time to volley the next shot coming at you. The fact is, if your opponent puts enough pace on it, the ball may get back to you before you reach the service line. That's why it's so important to practice transition volleys and half volleys.

Keep in mind that when coming to the net it's not a race. Remember what the great basketball coach, John Wooden said, "Be quick but don't hurry." If you rush, you're more likely to use only your hands and it becomes very hard to move laterally.

When you are in "no man's land" be sure to use your feet, stepping into your volleys or half volleys. Try to take the ball out of the air before it bounces because that is much easier than hitting a half volley.

Another thing I like to stress: Move forward. Too many players do just the opposite in that situation. They take a step back when they should be moving forward. I understand the logic. You think taking a step backward will give you more time. By the time you do that, though, you've opened the court up even more and worse, you're on your back foot which means you'll probably pop the ball up. Unless you've been lobbed, move forward.

If you have to hit the ball, try to hit a volley. Of course, if the ball lands at your feet, you're looking at a half-volley. (See Shot Making section.)

Is it possible to get better at handling no man's land? Here is one way you can improve your play in no man's land. Get with a partner and stand in no man's land and play to 10. Take turns feeding the first point and make the feeds as challenging as possible.

Learn to Play at the Net

If you want to avoid becoming a one dimensional player, becoming a good net player is a must. Think about the best doubles team you have ever played. I'll bet their net play was intimidating. You might even have worried a bit about being hit by the ball. Remember, it's much easier to win a point from the net than from the baseline! Here are 5 good reasons why:

1. You will receive most of the balls above the net
2. Your angles open up
3. You can hit down on the ball
4. You can close off the court better
5. You put pressure on the other team to come up with a great shot

As an instructor, I am well aware that many of my students are hesitant to come to the net, especially when they recognize that their net game isn't as good as their game at the baseline. When transitioning to the net you are going to make some mistakes, but with practice, your good shots will outweigh the bad.

Handling Advice

If you've been playing the game for a while, no doubt you get tips from a variety of people; coaches, partners, opponents and even a non-tennis playing spouse. Let's be honest here. We all love to coach others. The problem is it doesn't take very long to recognize that some tips you get conflict with other advice you've been offered.

If you try to follow every bit of advice you get you will surely wind up confused. It's okay to listen to the opinions of others, but you are ultimately responsible for determining what works best for you.

A woman I teach has been told by friends that she should stay behind the baseline as much as possible, when in fact, she might be better off coming to the net at every opportunity. Why? She has trouble hitting two decent groundstrokes in a row. Yet, because she is tall and has a wide reach, she is pretty effective when she does come to the net. When it comes to receiving advice about your tennis game, it makes sense to consider the source.

One thing that many tennis players find hard to accept is that it's virtually impossible to rush the process of learning a new stroke or strategy. It takes time and effort to make productive changes. It's true that a simple tip, like, "when serving, don't drop your tossing hand," can have an immediate affect on your play. Hopefully a positive one, but that is by no means guaranteed.

As a coach, I rarely offer my players tips that would require them to alter a stroke during a match because it puts them in a practice mindset which is likely to hurt their performance. In most cases repetition is the key to mastering changes in your game. There are no shortcuts.

Here is a case in point about teaching: I demonstrated the crosscourt rollover shot to Len in one of his first lessons. He remembered it but didn't feel comfortable actually trying to execute the shot until several years later.

There are several reasons why this can happen. Whether you get advice from your instructor during a lesson or from a bystander during a changeover, first and foremost you have to be ready to absorb it. You may not be skilled enough at the time you get the advice to take full advantage of it. Sometimes it's simply a lack of confidence on the player's part. In some instances it's not having the presence of mind, simply recognizing that "now is when you should be taking the shot."

Occasionally a player simply doesn't believe a particular tip will work for him. Beyond the basics, there are no hard and fast rules that determine when you should be able to hit certain shots or move to a particular spot on the court.

One of the things that can drive a teaching pro to distraction is explaining the same technique over and over again and not seeing the player make meaningful progress. Other tennis instructors say the same thing. As much as I hate to admit it, sometimes it might be my fault. The fact is coaches have to be very patient with their students. I have learned to rephrase what I say, recognizing that different players respond to different ways of describing aspects of the game.

Bottom line: Be a student of the game. Then take responsibility for the outcome.

Serve and Volley

The serve and volley is practically a lost art in singles because players focus a great deal more on developing groundstrokes rather than volleys. As a result, players are capable of hitting stronger returns. In doubles however, it's still a must for several reasons. When you serve and volley you're putting pressure on the returner to hit a great shot to start the rally. After you serve and then come to the net, you begin to close the court off. If your opponent returns with a floater, it's likely the point will not end in her favor.

The second reason to serve and volley is tactical. As I discuss elsewhere in the book, you must be able to adapt to different playing styles. Serve and volley is a great tactic. For example, if you are playing someone who is a backboard, a player who has the knack of returning every shot you hit, you have to get to the net or you will die a slow death from the baseline.

Another reason is to add variety to your game. If you rarely serve and volley, the element of surprise is awesome. Returners can get complacent. If you hang back, returners know that all they have to do is get the ball back crosscourt. Sneaking in every now and then will get you some easy points and helps to keep your opponent off balance.

Lastly, a serve and volley maneuver is ideal if you need a short point. Many times you'll play several long and grueling points which take the wind out of you. When you serve and volley you won't get into a twenty shot rally which can help you conserve energy

You make a decision to serve and volley before you start the point. You can't hit a serve and then say, "I'm going in," because it's too late. Here a few keys elements to help you succeed.

- Don't worry about the pace of your serve. The harder you hit it, the faster it will be returned to you. Spin can be a great option to help you execute, since it will slow the ball down and make it tricky for the returner.
- Split step or get set before your opponent hits the return. Most players want to start from the baseline and get to the middle of the service box for their first volley. In a perfect world that would be great, but it rarely happens. Most players only get to take about three steps before they have to prepare for the shot coming back. Be sure not to rush unless you get a floating return.
- Location, location, location. Where you place your serve is key. The body or the "T" is great since it will limit angles. You can serve out wide but it must be very

well placed so that your opponent is stretching for the serve and not able to set up.

- Don't feel like you have to end the point on the first volley. Sometimes it will happen, but remember the height of the ball will determine how aggressive you can be.

Most players prefer to serve and volley on a first serve, but it is a smart choice on your second serve as well. Your serve will have less pace and it also helps create an element of surprise. When you begin to practice serve and volley, remember to be relentless. There's only one way to get better and that is to practice, make mistakes and take chances.

The Mental Game

Mental Toughness

It isn't always easy to relax and have fun. Things go wrong on the tennis court. That's where mental toughness comes into play. Mental toughness and the determination to persevere no matter what's happening on the court, or in your life at the moment, truly separates consistent winners from average players. Mental toughness is really about having the will to face obstacles without letting them derail your game. Mental toughness doesn't guarantee you'll win, but with it, you won't lose because you gave in or gave up because of an unexpected problem.

Let me give you some examples of unanticipated problems. Have you ever played someone who makes bad line calls? I have seen many players over the years melt down after an alleged bad line call. By the time they regain their composure, several games have gone by and now they're losing, or the momentum has shifted drastically.

It's windy, you're feeling tired and you don't have your "A" game going for you today. There are many situations that are less than ideal. Mental toughness, persistence in the face of adversity, can help you push through these problems.

During every match you play, something will go wrong. Your attitude about mistakes can dramatically affect your confidence and your play. You must learn to be indifferent to errors committed in the moment. That moment is gone. You cannot get it back. Certainly, you may feel bad about missing an easy shot, but it serves no purpose to let your opponent see how you feel. Focus on what you are going to do on the next point, or think about where you have won points previously. Don't waste time and energy thinking about one bad shot.

I believe the best way to improve your mental toughness is to play more matches particularly in tournaments or leagues. In practice and clinics it's impossible to cover every scenario.

One potential problem with playing more tournament matches is that some players put too much importance on individual wins and losses. The important thing is that you learn from your losses, so that the next time you are in a tough spot you are better prepared to handle the situation. A great example: How well do you do facing a break point on your serve? It's a scenario we all have to face, but once you've had this happen enough times, you won't panic. You remember what have you've done in the past to get out of this situation.

In my experience, there are some drills that can strengthen a player's mental toughness, such as 3 to win a major, down 30 love or even placing different values on points. Suggested drills can be found in the last section of the book.

Things to Avoid on Game Day

When it comes to preparation and play, there are some behaviors you should strive to avoid. Let's take a look at five important ones.

1. Don't let the first three games of a match affect your attitude for the duration of the set or worse, the match. Not everyone is a fast starter. If you're down 3-0 or 2-1, the set is not over unless you quit. All sports have momentum swings. Sometimes all you have to do is hang in there long enough for momentum to swing in your direction. In the 1984 French Open final, Ivan Lendl was down two sets to zero. He had to win three straight sets to take the match from John McEnroe, who was in the midst of a 39 match winning streak. Lendl won the match because he never quit that day. Neither should you.
2. Strings get loose or break, grips come apart and even rackets break. Even your sneakers can be a source of misery. These are all fixable problems. Like going to the dentist or getting your oil changed, tennis equipment maintenance is an unavoidable part of life. You wouldn't take a cross country road trip without making sure your car is ready for the journey. Why would you go into a match without making sure your equipment is in tip-top shape? At a minimum, you should have two good rackets with you when you play. You should be able to change your grip (overwrap) ideally in 60 seconds or less during a changeover.
3. Avoid the wrong foods. Not being smart about what you eat can affect your energy level and your ability

to focus. If you don't eat enough you run the risk of being too weak to compete. If you overeat, your ability to move can be compromised. For solid advice on the right way to eat check the USTA Web site. When I was playing in junior tournaments, my mother used to give me M&M Peanuts to snack on. I always ate the green ones because the local legend at the time was they were lucky. While I don't recommend candy, it's probably better than nothing. I do recommend you bring a power bar or banana to a match. Eat foods you know work well for you. No experimenting.

4. Failure to warm up before a match can be costly. Even if time is tight, riding a bike for five minutes to loosen up is helpful. I also notice that most adults don't hit enough practice serves prior to a match. When your muscles aren't loose and your mind isn't properly focused, it can cost you several games.

Learn to Handle Stress

Tennis is often a stressful game. The rules of the game, the dimensions of the court, the short duration of each point and each game, combine to induce stress. Most tennis players tend to play against players with similar skills. A player who learns to handle stress properly will win more matches especially against someone who allows stress to affect their play.

Some players like to play fast. Others prefer a more deliberate pace. Either way, when you're serving and it isn't going well, slow down. When you're losing the other guy is usually eager to keep the game moving along at a faster pace. Slowing down the pace of the game is almost like a timeout in basketball. It helps to break your opponent's momentum and gives you time to refocus on what you need to do.

Players are often tempted to rush things when they're behind in the match. They want to get back on track and regain the lead. They take bigger risks. They lose patience, going for too much before they have their adversary on defense. That's a bad strategy, or maybe it's the absence of one. Instead, put your mind to work.

What do you think about between points? Whether you're thinking about the clean winner you just hit, or the fact that you just hit the ball long again, that's a problem. If you're serving, you should be thinking about the other guy's weaknesses.

You want to experiment with your serve placement. Figure out how well they hit the ball when it isn't in the strike zone, (knee to waist.) Can they handle a kick serve? How about a slice that forces them to bend their knees? Check to see how they respond when you take them out wide, or serve to the body. As the match progresses, you'll have a better sense of what your opponent's capabilities are and what's working for you. Focus on where you want the ball to go to get the point started.

There are tactics you can employ to buy a little extra time to think between points. For example, you can pick up your towel and wipe perspiration off. Jimmy Connors went to his towel 66 times in his match with Aaron Krickstein in the 1991 US Open Quarterfinals. It was excessive, but you get the point.

If you're receiving serve, you play at the server's pace, but usually you have some time to think about your strategy. When it comes to returning a first serve, a lot of players only want to keep the ball in play. That's fine, but your goal should be to hit the ball using the longest part of the court. On second serve, you need to know exactly what you plan to do *before the serve is even hit*. There simply isn't enough time between the first and second serve to strategize.

Changeovers give you another chance to reduce stress. First of all, sit down. During an official match, you have 90 seconds. Use that time to review the last couple of games. How did you win your points? Was there a particular shot, or strategy that won you some points? Or, was it as simple as your opponent making unforced errors? Consider how you lost points as well. Did your opponent hit winners? Did you make some unforced errors?

What's the score? If you're down three games, it's time to change your strategy. If you're up 3-0, keep doing what you're doing. Now is not the time to experiment.

Use the time between points and on changeovers wisely. Don't waste precious moments berating yourself over your last shot, or worrying about the score. Think strategically and win more often.

A Winning Attitude Part 1

Obviously when it comes to having a winning attitude there is no substitute for being well prepared and in good physical shape. But there's more to it than that. There's a fine line between being cocky and being confident. When you step onto the court do you expect to win? If not, guess what? You're probably going to lose. Your attitude determines the outcome of your matches far more often than you may realize.

Let's say that during the warm-up you realize you are about to play someone who is simply a better player. You start thinking you have to have the game of your life to win. The pressure is mounting before the match gets underway. If you are playing someone "stronger" you have to make them play. You can't go out guns blazing and hit the ball harder or to more specific targets than normal. You have to play your game and make them earn their victory. If they hit winners, at least they earned it. You didn't hand it to them by giving up without a fight.

Understand that objectively speaking, there will be days when you are matched with a player more skilled than you are. But as they say about the NFL, on any given Sunday, even the lowliest team can beat the best team in the league.

One way to overcome doubts is to know what you do best. For example, a player who knows his strengths and says, "My serve and my inside out forehand are my two biggest strengths. If I do these two things well today, I can beat anybody," is much more likely to win.

You don't need to imitate Mohammad Ali, announcing to everyone who will listen, that you're going to win. But, do tell *yourself* you're going to win and believe it.

I coach a highly ranked 16-year-old junior player who honestly believes he can beat anybody. If Roger Federer showed up on his court, he would think he could take Roger! Having a no-nonsense, positive attitude like that can only help you on the court.

While trash talking before the match isn't necessary, your body language, the way you walk onto the court, does matter. Even if your opponent doesn't consciously notice your confident demeanor, chances are, on some level it will affect them.

Winning Attitude Part 2

While a good attitude is critical to playing winning tennis, unfortunately, some players have traits that lead to poor outcomes. You get tired. Things start to go wrong on the court or maybe you've already had a bad day even before you get to the court. These traits, habits really, can be corrected if you're willing to recognize them and work to reduce, if not eliminate them. Here are three common player types. From time to time, we're all guilty of these traits. The key is recognizing it during a match and righting the ship.

The Critic

This is the player who has to nitpick every shot, even when she wins the point. She wasn't satisfied with the ball's placement, won the point only because her adversary was out of position, etc. She has a comment, usually negative, for every point she plays.

"You're playing lousy tennis today."

"Move your feet!"

"How could you miss that shot?"

First of all, you won't remember these remarks. Making them won't help you fix your game. Worse, beating yourself up actually reduces the likelihood of improving your performance. Negative talk also gives encouragement to your opponent. The player who says something negative after every shot will soon be labeled a head case.

The Anger Management Candidate

How many times have you really played better when you were angry? Not too many, right? I suppose I've seen a handful of people play better angry, but it's rare. Let's take a look at what happens when you get angry:

- You focus on the cause of your anger rather than the task at hand. Before you know it, two or three points have been played and you're not really there.
- You begin to feel embarrassed by your behavior, another unwelcome distraction.
- You spend a lot of energy that could be put to productive use.

Anger on the tennis court is never a pretty sight. It just isn't productive. I'll never forget the time my opponent in a USTA Juniors match hit a ball into the net. He was so angry he threw his racket into the fence. We were only about a minute into our warm up! Guess who won the match? Some players get angry at their opponent, usually for something small.

Maybe the player thought his opponent made a bad call, or he didn't like the way the guy gave him the balls.

It's important to recognize that anger directed toward your opponent might well be misplaced. You may be in a bad mood to begin with, or angry because you're playing poorly. Either way, it's a recipe for disaster. When I see someone getting angry at their opponent, I know the match is probably over. He's now playing his opponent, not the game of tennis.

The Excuse Meister

This player is an excuse making machine. When he loses a match, it is NEVER because of the way *he* played. His strings were loose, it was too windy, the sun was brutal, the line calls favored his opponent, his wrist was hurting or his shoulder was sore. Listen, if your strings really are loose, isn't that something you should address before you play? If you have an injury that's serious enough to affect your play, maybe it's best to have a medical checkup before you play again.

Don't be this guy. Aside from damaging your credibility, making excuses all but eliminates the opportunity to evaluate your game so you can make improvements. Every time you play you will face at least one challenge in addition to your opponent. Learn to deal with these obstacles and overcome them. Even a few professional tennis players fall into the excuse trap. They make frequent coaching changes or they blame their schedule for their poor play. The bottom line is that until a player accepts responsibility for his level of play, it is very hard to make the changes necessary to become a better player.

If you want to be a good tennis player, learn how to lose a point. It might help to remember that you will win some points that are, pure and simple, a gift. You shank an overhead and the tennis gods make it a winner. Anyone who plays tennis, from the beginner to the world's number one ranked player, will lose some points. The good ones understand that. They let it go and move on.

Shot Making Core Shots

Grip Options

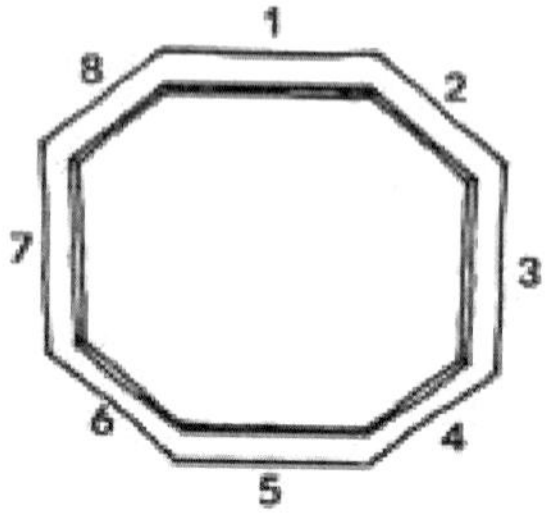

Before you can master your core shots you must become very familiar with almost all of the grips types. When referring to grip placement use your bottom knuckle on your dominant hand and place it on the appropriate number above. All rackets have eight sides or bevels for a reason.

stages.

- The traditional eastern grip (or handshake grip) is used by many for a forehand and is the easiest to master.

Your index finger's base (or bottom) knuckle is placed on panel 3 of your racket. Most players are taught this grip when they first start playing tennis. The disadvantage with this grip is you will not get as much topspin as the other grips because the face of the racket will only be slightly closed. If you use this grip for other shots you would be wise to keep reading as again this grip has its limitations

- The semi western forehand grip is the grip of choice for more advanced players, including touring pros. It's achieved by placing your index finger's base knuckle on panel 4. In essence, it closes the face of your racket more, which in turn gives you great topspin. This to me is the grip of choice because it gives great topspin and is not too extreme. The disadvantage of this grip is that it does take more time to change grips during a point since it's lower than an eastern grip. Also, it is not to the right grip for extremely low balls.
- The western forehand grip is the most extreme of the grips. It requires you to put your index finger's base knuckle at panel 5. I've never taught anyone this grip for a few reasons. One is that too much topspin is a bad thing. With excessive topspin your balls may land too short in the court and you will lose pace as well. Another reason is this grip can stress your elbow if used over long periods of time. Lastly, since your grip has now moved even lower on your racket, changes during a point take even more time. Again, it becomes extremely challenging to hit low balls.
- The Continental grip could be the most important grip of them all. This is the grip everyone should use

for serves, overheads, volleys and slice shots. Many people are not taught this from day one and there's a reason. This grip requires good wrist strength and feeling comfortable adjusting your racket angle to open or close the racket face based on the shot. This only comes from lots and lots of practice. With this grip, you must place only your base knuckle on your index finger on panel number 2 having your remaining (middle, ring and pinky) fingers hanging below at a slight angle. Many players line all their fingers up with panel number 2 and it becomes more difficult and uncomfortable. Some people refer to this grip as the hammer grip since it's a similar feeling. If this is a grip you are not familiar with, I would make this a top priority.

Open or Closed Stance?

For many years tennis was played almost exclusively with a closed stance. As the speed of the game changed, thanks to better conditioning and technology advances, players moved to an open stance for ground strokes. An open stance allows for quicker preparation and faster hip movement which helps generate pace and therefore power.

With a closed stance your body is sideways, your chest facing the sidelines. With an open stance your chest faces the opposite side of the court. Whether to hit with an open or closed stance is a common topic of debate these days. Some say the game is too fast now to use a closed stance but that really depends on your level of play. How many people do you play that can hit with pace like a pro would? Not many I'll bet.

In my opinion, it only helps your game if you learn to hit with both an open and closed stance. Let's take a look at the advantages of each:

Closed stance

A closed stance lengthens your strike zone because now you can make contact anywhere from slightly behind your front foot to a spot in front of it. It's also much easier to disguise where you plan to put the ball. Since so many players hit with an open or partially open stance today, a closed stance often suggests the player is going down the line. Naturally, a closed stance does make it easier to hit the ball down the line. Yet, by rotating your hips fully through the shot you can easily hit the ball crosscourt. A closed stance is a must if you want to hit effective approach shots.

Open stance

One of the great advantages of an open stance is that it allows for quicker preparation, critical when you're returning a ball with a lot of pace on it. You can also put more pace on the balls you hit. An open stance is also a way to shorten the time it takes to get the ball over the net when you're returning serves.

Learn to hit with both open and closed stances on forehands and backhands. The choice of when to hit open or closed is situational, but it's fair to say the more pace on the ball coming at you the more likely you'll want to use an open stance. An open stance can be great for return of serves and shots that are made on the outside portion of the court, but are not limited to those situations.

The Serve

I find that many players can be very stubborn about their serve. When your first serve is working, there is nothing wrong with sticking with it. Enjoy every moment of it. When it's not working though, you can save yourself a lot of heartache and maybe even the match if you will start using your second serve on your first serve. How do you know when it's time to switch? When you're down two points (0-30 or 15-40 for example) you have lost the right to hit your first serve. You are now on "first serve probation" until you get the score back to even.

Perhaps the most important thing you can do to improve your serve is to recognize that effective serve placement will win you far more points than pace. The goal is not to hit as hard as you can. Just like your forehand, figure out what your number is and stick with it. Having a variety of serves at your disposal is essential to winning more matches. Let's review the three types of serve.

Flat Serve

The flat serve can be your best friend if you happen to be on that day, meaning your timing is great and you're getting the pace and placement you want. When things are going well, you're probably getting a lot of easy points and even an occasional ace. The bad news is there is little room for error with the flat serve. When it's not working, many players are left with a weak second serve, or worse, double faults. Ideally, you should use a continental grip to hit the flat serve, but many players use an eastern, or even a semi-western grip.

When you use a continental grip to hit a flat serve, you must pronate your wrist to square your racket face, which makes it easier to snap/collapse your wrist. Note that when you grip the racket, there should be a space between your middle and index finger, large enough to fit another finger. This space between your fingers alleviates pressure on your wrist and allows you bring your racket head down quickly. This is referred to as your trigger finger.

Your toss should be in line with your hitting shoulder, about 3 inches above where you will make contact. The ball should be a few inches into the court. You may have been taught to toss the ball higher, but I find that when the ball is tossed too high, you may be vulnerable to weather conditions like the sun and wind. And, tossing the ball too high may interrupt your service motion, reducing your momentum. Your follow through on the flat serve is down and tight toward your leading leg.

A flat serve is a useful weapon, but for most players it isn't reliable enough to count on in every match or situation.

Slice serve

To be an effective server, you must develop a slice serve. Most returners learn how to adjust for pace, but it isn't nearly as easy to handle a serve that is moving away from you or, is coming into your body. Handling a slice serve requires the returner to move, which often reduces the effectiveness of the return. If you don't already have a slice serve, work to develop one. By the way, when you hit a slice serve as a first serve it will often surprise your opponent.

Some players use an eastern or semi-western grip to hit a slice serve. I can tell you without hesitation, that you will get better results with a continental grip. The key with this serve is to be sure to toss the ball outside your hitting shoulder so you can make contact on the side of the ball. Sweep the racket across your body with your follow through so your racket finishes at your opposite hip.

As you learn the slice serve, you may discover that the ball is going wide left. Don't be discouraged. Simply aim to the right of your target to allow the ball to work from right to left, much like a draw in golf, pronate your wrist. Note to left-handers: If you don't have a slice serve, you must develop one. Your opponents will hate it, because the ball does the opposite of what they are used to seeing.

Kick Serve

The kick serve is one of the most difficult shots to hit in tennis, but players who can master it often have a tremendous advantage over their opponents. Simply said, a kick serve puts top spin on your serve. It is usually used as a second serve. When done properly, the ball kicks high and to the right after landing in the service box which is out of your opponent's strike zone.

Another advantage of the kick serve is you won't miss it long very often. You can be confident you won't double fault. Once the ball is over the net, it sinks quickly. So how do you hit a kick serve?

- A continental grip is a must.
- Toss the ball at eleven o'clock, slightly behind your left shoulder. As you get more proficient you can start to move your toss further back to around 9 o'clock dropping the racket head lower.

- Your service motion runs left to right from behind your left shoulder. Be sure to take your racket back lower than a flat or slice serve.
- Strike the underside of the ball, brushing it forward which should send the ball higher over the net than a flat serve.
- For maximum effectiveness arch your back as you toss the ball in the air.
- Your racket head speed should be the same as it is on your first serve.
- Hit the kick serve only after you've warmed up. It's definitely not your first serve of the day.

How do you know you've hit a solid kick serve? When you're practicing, after the ball lands in the service box, does it hit either the back or side fence? If it does, that's a great kick serve. Do it in a match and it's often a nightmare for your opponent.

Have a Routine When You Serve

Most of us have routines that we rarely vary. For some of us, it's coffee first thing in the morning. Going to bed every night at the same time, eating meals at set times of day or exercising daily are all routines, and they serve an important purpose. Having a routine helps us to stay on task. There are so many distractions literally at our fingertips.

Nearly every professional tennis player on tour has a serving routine. They do this because it minimizes distractions like negative thoughts. In stressful moments, having a routine can have a calming effect.

Here's my serving routine. I set my feet first. Then I bounce the ball exactly three times. Make eye contact with the returner just long enough to verify he's ready. I'm also selecting my target. In fact my only thought during my routine is where I'm going to put the ball. I take a deep breath to relax my muscles, especially my serving arm. Then I serve.

Whatever your serving routine is, be sure to reinforce it when you practice serves. Don't be one of those players who hits serve after serve in practice as if the goal was to be the first one to empty the ball hopper. Go through your routine on every serve. Remember, a regular routine gives you a reliable rhythm no matter what's happening in the match.

Dictate Points with Your Serve

There is a reason why professional tennis players hold serve so often. It helps to have a 120 mph serve, but that's not the only reason they hold so often. As we've discussed earlier, variety, such as different spins and placing the ball in different locations, help you to hold serve.

But serve placement also starts to determine the outcome of the point. That's why it's so important in doubles play to let your partner know where you plan to serve the ball. There are very few "always" or "never" situations in tennis, but the scenarios we will review here describe likely outcomes. For example, when you serve to the T, the ball typically comes back to the middle of the court. In this situation, your doubles partner closes at an angle toward the net strap, hoping to get his racket on the return.

What about a serve to the body? As you know, it tends to handcuff the returner, making it hard for her to follow through.

She is forced to more or less block the ball back. A side note about the body serve. It is an underused option. Maybe there are no aces there, but your partner will look like a hero putting the ball away over and over again.

Serving wide is the other option. The results are less predictable because your adversary can choose to go crosscourt, or down the line. Note however, that it is a lot easier to return the wide serve crosscourt. In this situation, your partner covers the line. That's not to say that your partner stands in the alley. You can't afford to overcommit and make it impossible to make a play on a ball near the center of the court.

Consistently being able to put the ball where you want it requires practice. The rewards are worth the effort. Serve placement can dictate the entire point. When you decide where to hit your serve, take into account your opponent's strengths and weaknesses. For example, if he has a weak backhand, serving out wide (on the add side for right-handed players) probably means a weak or even failed return. Consider too that most players have a strike zone the same way baseball players do. If you happen to possess a reliable kick serve, the high bounce can keep most players off balance. Some players like balls waist high so they can hit a solid cross court forehand return. Others, crave opportunities to crush a backhand down the line. Keeping the ball out of your opponent's strike zone is an important element of your serving strategy. Slice serves tend to come in handy when you're playing a taller person who may not bend, or move away from the ball as well.

A good server also knows that changing pace on first and second serves can get excellent results. If your opponent is used to seeing a fast paced flat serve, slowing it down often causes him to get out too far ahead of the ball and hit it crosscourt wide of the line. Years ago I saw Juan Martin del Potro live at the US Open. I noticed that when serving from the add side he consistently added a bit of slice. If you saw it on TV it would seem he was hitting the ball flat. The slice was his way of adding a bit of variety to his first serve. It was a subtle maneuver. It was effective because it was hard for the receiver to judge. It is especially challenging for those who like to hit a forehand return since the ball was moving away from them. The bottom line is this: Have a plan when you decide which serve to hit.

First Serve Test

If you watch the pros play on TV you'll notice one statistic that commentators always show viewers. It's first serve percentage. Whether it's Mary Carillo or John McEnroe, they will point out that the player with the higher percentage of first serves in is more likely to win the match.

The majority of players I teach tend to overestimate their first serve percentage. Here's a simple test you can perform, one that will give you a good idea of the results you can expect in a match.

1. Start by warming up your serve until you are ready to hit first serves.
2. Hit 10 first serves, keeping count to see how many you get in. Repeat this several times, taking time between each serve as if you were in a match.
3. If you're first serve percentage is below 60%, practice your serve more often. On the other hand, if your

average is 80% or higher, you may want to be more aggressive and add pace to your serve. Keep in mind that the top pros on the tour today are getting about 65% of their first serves in on a good day. I just checked the stats for the Australian Open (2015) and the top 20 players ranged from 69% to 81%. Since that represents the top 20 players, shooting for 60% or more is realistic for most of us.

Return of Serve

The return of serve should be one of your most valuable shots. Yet, it is probably the most under practiced shot in tennis. Novak Djokovic, Andy Murray and hall of famer, Andre Agassi, considered by many to be the best returner of all time, know the importance of a strong return. You can improve your ability to return serves with practice. This is where having a good practice partner comes in handy. One of you serves until the returner misses 5 to 7 cross court returns. Then reverse roles.

If you want to hit a solid return, moving forward is a must. Too many returners move side to side or even worse, back up. When you move forward you can cut off the angle not to mention your return will get back to the server faster. Occasionally, you will be required to return a kick serve. It is a challenge to successfully return this serve, but it is something you can learn to do. As with any service return a split step is essential.

You then have two options. The key to success is you have to be willing to step forward and take the ball on the rise. It requires practice to master the timing. Once you hit the ball you will probably be standing in no-man's land. You must quickly decide whether to continue to the net or return to the baseline.

If hitting on the rise won't work for you, step back behind the baseline and wait for the ball to come down before hitting it. Your return in that situation will be strictly a defensive shot.

The next time you watch a professional tennis tournament notice how far back the returner stands waiting for the serve. Then take note of how far they move up when they actually make contact with the ball. Don't be stubborn about where you stand to return serve. You may have to adjust due to spin, pace or lack thereof.

If you are a recreational player you should also practice returning the dink serve. Mostly used as a second serve, this is a ball that arrives without much pace and tends to be short, meaning you have to come up into the service box to hit your return. All tennis pros will tell you to take advantage of the second serve.

This is why first serve percentage is so important. When players are getting a low percentage of their first serves in, there are many opportunities to score points off a weak second serve. Since the ball will likely be short, an effective way to handle the return of a dinky serve is to treat it like an approach shot. A good approach shot requires hitting the ball farther out in front of you than normal. Your follow through is lower than it is with a ground stroke. Visualize hitting the ball six inches above the net.

Remember you're standing in no-man's land so it's important to place the ball to your maximum advantage. In singles, try to hit the ball down the line. In doubles you have several options. You can hit the ball right back at the server, down the line or at a sharp crosscourt angle.

It might take a few misses before you get your timing down, but don't give up. Hitting an aggressive shot sends a message.

The Forehand

If you're reading this book I'm going to assume you know how to hit this shot. Still, it's worth a little bit of time to review the things you need to do to strengthen your forehand.

1. There are several grips you can use to hit a forehand. Which one you use depends on your level of play. Grip options are discussed in more detail later in the topspin section. I encourage beginners to start with an eastern grip, holding the racket with the base of your palm, at the end of the butt cap. When you've been playing for a while, you begin to see the value and importance of control and spin. Usually that leads players toward a semi-western grip. This transition can be gradual. If you've been playing for a while, you'll recall that as you gained confidence you moved your hand perhaps one-half bevel over at first. Some experienced players will even use a western grip but I discourage it because it requires excessive grip changes as you go between forehand and backhand strokes. Although you can get maximum spin with a western grip, you're likely to sacrifice pace and depth in the process. Even worse, the western grip can cause elbow problems.

2. How do you prepare? What do you do with your non-dominant hand? Many players set up with the hand extended in front. That's fine, but if you want more power, get your non-dominant hand closer to your racket. As you get your hand closer to your racket it forces your body to turn. Many players on tour even hold their racket with their non-dominant hand near the throat as they take it back. Just watch next time the pros are playing.
3. Use your shoulder. When you finish most ground strokes, your elbow should be away from your body. If your elbow finishes near the center of your chest, you are not using your shoulder. This is a very common mistake which hinders pace and placement. Remember a good forehand should be a full swing. Maintain a lighter grip pressure and have some bend in your elbow will allow you to execute a full swing. You don't want to slam on the brakes after contact. If you use your shoulder it will also be easier on your elbow for all those out there with elbow issues. If your shoulder is stiff or sore the day after a match I don't consider that a bad thing. I would love to tell you that prior to a match I stretch for 15 minutes, but I don't. I will tell you that I focus on stretching my shoulder by either doing some easy windmills or turning the back of my hand outward so that it's facing the fence. Then I slowly apply pressure with a straight arm against the fence.
4. Learn to load, explode and land correctly. Loading is transitioning your weight to your back leg with a good knee bend. Exploding is pushing with your toes,

> starting to come out of your knee bend and using your hips and shoulders to apply the energy you loaded to (throw your weight) meet the ball at contact. Landing is what happens after you hit the ball. If you've loaded and exploded properly, you will land on your left foot, with most, if not all you weight on it. To put it simply, you want to LOAD, EXPLODE and LAND! Most really good tennis players don't have pretty feet. With enough repetition, you will notice calluses on your big toe and on the outside of the balls of your feet. Sorry for the bad news.

If you currently have an eastern grip and want to make a change to a semi western, I would make it gradually. What I mean by this is start by moving your knuckle to the lowest part of panel 3 before going to panel 4 for the semi western. This transition might give you a little more success since you're used to laying your wrist back at a slightly different angle with your eastern grip. With a grip change there may also be a learning curve in the angle you lay your wrist back at contact.

Topspin

In the game of tennis, topspin is "King." One of the best feelings you will ever have in tennis is taking a full, aggressive swing from anywhere in the court, knowing that there's no way it's going out. That's the beauty of topspin. Topspin puts a forward rotation on the ball, usually creating an arc in your ball flight, which allows the ball to descend quickly thus landing in the court with good force.

Other than being able to swing more aggressively and keep more balls in play, topspin is also great for getting the ball out of your opponent's strike zone. With forward rotation, the ball comes crashing down, thus jumping up much higher than a flat ball. To me, this is a huge advantage because most players are good at hitting balls waist high. Hitting a ball that arrives shoulder high is considerably more difficult. Topspin puts your opponent on defense.

Now that we know the advantages of topspin, how are we going to accomplish producing topspin? No doubt you've heard someone say, "To achieve topspin you must brush up on the ball." I've said it too, but there's more to it than just brushing up on the back of the ball. For starters you must lower your racket with a closed racket face below the ball to achieve the desired effect. Secondly, you do brush up on the back of the ball but only for a split second. Those who only brush up will generate topspin, but maybe end up with their racket on the right side of their body too long, losing pace and depth. To be effective at topspin, you must brush and then roll. What I mean by this is after you brush up on the ball, your racket face must start to close instead of staying open after brushing up. You do this by using your wrist in a sideways waving motion.

A good visual would be you pressing a ball up against the net tape brushing it up to get it over the net and then, using a hand-wrist action, rolling it over on to the other side of the tape. To practice this, you could start on the service line and begin to brush up and roll over balls so that they land in the service box on the other side of the net. As you practice this you will notice that the faster you move your wrist the more topspin you will produce. I suggest starting very slowly with your wrist, using what I would call a lazy motion.

Are there certain shots that should have more topspin? When we are talking about ground strokes, I would use heavy to moderate spin depending on your desired depth. More spin will make your strokes land shorter unless you aim much higher above the net. Approach shots should typically use less topspin since you need to keep the ball lower to the net and you want to get the ball quickly to your opponent. Down the line passing shots should also have less topspin since speed helps to get the ball past your opponent. Crosscourt passing shots are a different matter. You need the ball to drop quickly since there is less room to land the ball. Most players speed up the wrist in this situation. Lobs can vary with topspin but I prefer a lot of spin because a poorly executed lob with heavy spin can still be very difficult to return.

So far we have been talking about the forehand but what about the backhand? If you use a standard grip on this stroke and you get below the ball, chances are you already put some topspin on your backhand. I don't teach a different grip in this situation because most players already lack power on their backhand. By making an aggressive grip change for topspin, they will lose even more pace. If you use a two-handed backhand, I would suggest you use your left wrist the same way you would on your forehand. When you practice this you will see if you really use your non dominant hand to hit your backhand.

Topspin is truly important to your game. If you don't currently use it, or don't feel comfortable with it, I would suggest making this a top goal. The only warning I have about topspin would be don't force it. For most players the ball needs to be at least knee high. If the ball is extremely low remember your goal is to get it over the net and a closed racket face makes that very difficult.

The Backhand

It's no secret that a lot of players struggle when it comes to their backhand stroke. Even advanced players can run into problems. I encourage players to use a two-handed backhand whenever possible. While there are advantages to the one-handed backhand, a two-handed backhand is a better bet for most players.

First, the bad news: Unlike the one-handed backhand, using two hands doesn't allow you as much freedom with your hands and arms. You don't have as much reach and you need good footwork. That said, a two-handed backhand makes it easier to hit top spin and hit with power. Also, it's easier to hit high bouncing balls with a two-handed backhand. Returning serve is easier as well because you have the strength and support of a second hand, which is very important when dealing with a big server.

Five actions you can take to improve your two-handed backhand:

1. Let your non-dominant hand do the striking. Apply more pressure to that hand. If you want to get a feel for how much grip pressure you should use, hit some forehands with your other hand. That will give you an excellent feel for how much pressure you need. You use your non-dominant hand to impart spin on the ball as well.

2. Be sure both arms are loose. If you hit right-handed keep your left elbow bent. Between points you can shake your arms or let them dangle. Keep your elbows close to your body rather than straight out in front of you.
3. If you want to generate pace you have to use your hips. Keep your hips aligned with the racket's forward motion. If your hips are behind the racket or in front of it, you will sacrifice power and accuracy.
4. Have a friend check out your swing's finish. No doubt you've been told to finish this stroke over your shoulder. Let me add one clarification. Your racket should be ABOVE your shoulder, not on it. A good two-handed backhand requires a big, full swing. There's no touch with this shot.
5. Use your non-dominant hand to change the grip on your dominant hand so the racket face closes.

Some of you may be more comfortable with a one-handed backhand. That's fine as long as you accept the one-handed stroke's limitations. While you do have more reach and can get better placement using one hand, the reality is you will not overpower many with this stroke. Passing crosscourt is also a challenge for one-handers. A few pointers:

1. Proper set up is essential. Your legs play a very important role. You load your weight much like you do with your forehand, but you must bend your knees to generate power.
2. Your finish has to be long. When you finish, your racket is outside your hitting shoulder.
3. Use your wrist to brush up on the ball to get top spin.

The Perfect Lob

What makes a good lob? If the ball is at its highest point when it reaches your opponent's service line, you've done a good job! A lob is a touch shot. Using a lighter grip pressure, similar to a volley or drop shot is essential to hitting successful lobs. A looser grip allows the ball to stay on your racket longer, which improves your control and the chances you will place the ball where you want it.

Follow through is also very important to hitting an effective lob shot. Imagine your follow through as going up a ladder leaning against a wall. While your follow through winds up on your opposite shoulder as it would for a forehand stroke, it is more of an up and out motion.

By all means, avoid the short popping motion with a tight grip. Occasionally it works, but it's hard to consistently replicate and poor placement is a frequent result.

A lob can be an excellent offensive shot. Lobbing high to your opponent's backhand side puts them on the defensive. In doubles, lobbing on the net player's side of the court can force them to switch sides which may well result in one or both of your opponents being out of position. Offensive lobs should be hit on the second serve or, on a controllable ball, i.e., one that lacks depth and pace and is likely to bounce twice on your side of the court.

One of the most obvious lob situations occurs when you've been pulled off the court or backed into a corner out of position. In other words, you're on defense. A good lob buys you time to get into position and back into the point. Lobs can be great momentum killers. Say you've lost 2-3 points in a row. A well-placed lob can change momentum, force your opponent to move more and generate his own pace.

There are, of course, different types of lobs. One of my favorites is what I call the "sneaky lob." The ball's highest point is still at your opponent's service line but it's not as loopy and doesn't have the high arc most lobs have. But the ball gets to the other side quickly. With less height, it's harder to move around to hit an overhead. It forces your opponent to hit the hardest shot in tennis, the high backhand.

To gain the maximum advantage with your lobs, try to land the ball on your adversary's back hand side. To hit this shot, your follow through is even more outward than on a traditional lob before winding up with the racket on your opposite shoulder.

Another very useful lob to have in your arsenal is the top spin lob. To hit a good top spin lob you have to have the right ball to hit. Ideally it has to sit up, waist high. I recommend a semi-western grip for this shot. You must brush up on the ball using more racket head speed than you would for a traditional lob.

How frequently should you employ the lob? If you hit a couple of lobs early in a match, you will soon know whether your opponent is skilled and confident when it comes to hitting overheads. If you uncover a weakness in this area, the lob can be a productive offensive shot.

Yes, You Can Hit an Effective Overhead!

When faced with returning a lob, does your body language scream, "Oh no! I hate this shot. I never hit a good one." The Overhead is one of the most "mental shots" in tennis. Yet, many times I've seen players get a tremendous confidence boost from hitting a solid overhead. On the other hand, miss a couple of overheads and a player's confidence in the shot evaporates.

After missing one or two overheads some players become hesitant and fail to follow through. Instead they block the ball back, or use an abbreviated follow through. Not only is the shot likely to be weak, your opponent will recognize you've lost confidence. When that happens you can expect more lobs to come your way.

Like every shot in tennis, the overhead requires a lot of practice. Yet, few players spend enough time working on this shot. Expecting to hit a good one during a match without proper practice and preparation is foolhardy.

If you're having problems hitting an effective overhead, ask yourself, "Am I hitting the ball too hard?" This is a shot that should be hit at 80% of your full capacity. Also, ask yourself whether your grip pressure is too tight. If you grip the racket too tightly, your arm is too stiff to allow your elbow to bend as much as it should and your wrist won't snap properly. A looser grip will solve these problems, improving your chances of hitting an overhead that will make your opponent think twice before sending you another lob.

If you want to hit a good overhead, keep the ball in front of you by shuffling or sidestepping to get in the best position to hit the ball. Remember it's always easier to come back to the ball if you shuffle back too far. One thing I tell my students is act like a boxer; on your toes and bouncing around a bit as you get ready to hit this shot. Keeping the ball in front of you also allows you to hit down on the ball which will give you more pace and the desired feeling of a smash that will hit the court hard and bounce up high. Remember this is very similar to a serve but your contact point is further in front of you, which is much more doable since you're closer to the net.

Ideally, you want to return a lob while it's still in the air because it takes time away from your opponent. There are times however, when you should let the ball bounce before you hit it. If the ball is likely to land close to the net, let it bounce first so that you are not making contact on the other side of the net. Or, if the lob is extremely high, which can be hard to judge, let it bounce. The ball will bounce high, still giving you the opportunity to hit an overhead smash.

You should also learn to go both ways when hitting an overhead. Most players hit overheads cross court. But a good player must be able to turn and hit the ball in the opposite direction. To do that, turn your body and feet in the direction of the shot, your chest facing the target. By changing direction occasionally, you keep your opponents honest. They aren't sure where you will hit the ball.

The bottom line on an overhead is you must be able to do three things at once:

1. Turn, A good turn is essential to start the process of getting your feet into position by either shuffling, or using a cross over step. If you don't have to move your feet on an overhead, a miracle has just occurred.
2. Get your left arm up. Getting your left hand up, or your non hitting arm sounds easy enough, but I find that most players have it too low, many times below their head. This sounds like a small detail, but the higher your arm is up, the more upright your chin will be which will allow you to see the ball better. Having

your arm up should also help with your balance. Many players are taught to point at the ball. That's not a bad idea, but it's never helped me locate the ball.

3. Get your racket behind your head. Your right elbow should be bent. Most tennis players don't know what they look like when they hit the ball. That being said, many players don't bend their hitting elbow enough to allow for the power they desire.

Do these three things well and you'll be begging your opponent to go ahead and lob you.

There is one additional overhead that I feel is worth mentioning. The "scissor kick" is one that you will typically hit when your opponent hits a great lob, one that doesn't give you time to turn and run behind the ball.

The mechanics of this shot are very similar to a regular overhead. However, the footwork required to execute it makes this a very advanced shot. With the scissor kick you take a cross step (often called a carioca step) where your front foot steps across your back foot as you move backwards. Note that there is very little or even no shuffle, in this situation. This is because the ball is getting behind you very quickly.

How to hit a scissor kick overhead:

1. Turn sideways so your right leg is behind you with your racket up behind your head and your left arm raised skyward. As you move backwards, take a balanced step with your right leg, followed by a crossover, or carioca step with your left leg so you are prepared to jump.

2. When you jump your weight will be on your back foot. The jump must provide power as you accelerate your body to the ball.
3. As you swing at the ball, your right leg pushes up and your left leg kicks forward, hence the scissor motion. This will help you maintain your balance as you land on your left leg.
4. As with a normal overhead, remember your contact point with the ball is out in front of you. If you find you hit the ball long, you may not be accelerating enough.

If you can learn to hit this shot effectively, the scissor kick overhead can turn a defensive shot into an offensive shot.

The Approach Shot

The approach shot is one of the great separators in tennis. It can be the difference between taking control of the point and merely keeping the ball in play. Much like most tennis shots, your options are determined by the ball's height. Ideally you want to get to the ball at the peak of the bounce so you can be aggressive. If the ball gets below the net you may have lost an opportunity, or will need to use slice to stay on offense. The best players turn controllable balls into offense. Remember, a controllable ball is one without much pace that lands in the attack zone. After hitting this shot, you come to the net. During your match you should be on high alert looking for balls in this zone.

An approach can be hit with a semi-western, eastern or continental grip. When employing a slice approach shot you would use the continental grip. Although today's game is focused on power, for most players, it can be an effective shot. The beauty of a slice approach is that the ball stays low and it's a high percentage shot. In trying to return this ball your opponent is more likely to pop the ball up, giving you the chance to hit an overhead, or a high volley.

Use a semi-western grip when you have a ball that sits up and you want to hit a more powerful shot, perhaps directly at the player who is standing at the baseline in doubles or down the line in singles. Hit directly behind the ball, driving it to your opponent's control zone. Ideally, you want to hit this ball no more than six inches over the net.

If you want to hit successful approach shots, you must use a closed stance. Turn your body and shuffle, taking small side steps to the ball. As with most offensive shots, hit the ball further out in front of you. Note that approach shots should have less top spin. You want the ball to get there fast and stay low. In my experience, many players are uncomfortable with this shot. It's understandable because there is very little room for error. Remember you're hitting the approach from the attack zone. You've already cut off ¼ of the court, giving you less room to keep the ball in play.

That's why to hit this shot effectively; you have to alter your follow through as well. Instead of finishing shoulder high, you want to take the racket across your body waist high. If you finish high on your approach, you can count on the ball going long. With enough practice you can master this shot. When you do, you will win more often. If you don't feel confident with your approach shots, you need to make improving them a high priority. This is a fun shot to practice and the results can take you to another level quickly.

The Volley

When volleys come to mind, most tennis players, perhaps for good reason, picture themselves in the finishing zone. A volley, however, is any ball you take out of the air before the ball bounces, regardless of where you are on the court. (We'll discuss swinging volleys later.)

While volleys may not be a particularly gratifying shot for some players, if you can consistently hit them, you will win more matches.

A continental grip is the only grip you should be using when you hit a volley. If you use a semi-western or eastern forehand grip instead, low balls will find the net just about every time. In fact, I'm surprised by the number of people who use a forehand grip at the net. By using a continental grip, as you strike the ball, it imparts some backspin which helps enormously with placement and control. Grip pressure is critical as well. The tighter you squeeze, the less time the ball spends on the racket which results in depth, often more than you want. A looser grip pressure keeps the ball on the racket longer which deadens the ball.

The way to hit an effective volley:

1. Rest your right elbow against your ribcage (left if you're left handed.) This will give you more control and softer hands. Also, this will allow you to keep the ball out in front of you and keep you from swinging. There will not be an out-to-in on your motion.
2. Your hitting hand is extended in front of your body and your wrist is cocked to keep the racket out in front of you. For many players, laying the wrist back is difficult

because it's not a very natural feel, but it's a must to keep your racket out in front so that you don't swing. Also, it's quicker for set up, which is critical, especially when you are at the net and balls are getting to you more quickly.

3. Your stance is semi-closed.
4. Don't be afraid to scuff up your racket. I don't trust a tennis player with a perfect racket! Remember those plastic guards are replaceable. When it comes to half volleys, sometimes you will have to dig to get these shots.

Note that by angling the palm of your hand slightly skyward, you'll get more height on the ball and therefore depth. Players who volley well vary their pace, alternating between hard and soft volleys to fit the situation. If your opponent is at the baseline, you might hit a harder volley her way, following up with a soft volley that forces her to come to the net. It's an effective strategy.

Where should you place your volleys? It depends on the zone you're in. If you're in the control zone, (at or near the baseline) get the ball back as deep as possible. From the attack zone, your options start to open up. The ball's height will help you decide what to do.

If you're playing doubles and the ball is below the net, hit it back as deep as you can to the opponent that is farther from the net. If the ball is waist high, it's fine to go for an angle but be sure to take some pace off the ball. Finally, if the ball is above the net, hit it at your opponent's feet or, better yet, go behind them. In thirty plus year of tennis, I've never seen anyone run down a volley that got behind them.

You have the most options when you're in the finishing zone. The closer to the net you are the easier it is to hit angles. You can hit directly at your opponent (try to keep the ball low) if he is also at the net. Remember, ultimately, the height of the ball determines which options are likely to be successful. For example, if you are unfortunate enough to be in the finishing zone and the ball arrives below the net, hit to the deepest person on the court. If the ball is waist high, shoot for an angle, using less pace. If the ball is above the net, hit the ball directly at the net person's feet or behind them.

More on volleys:

- To reduce unforced errors, volley between your opponents.
- Change the pace of your volleys by using different grip pressures.
- Recognize that you will win more points at the net reducing pace, rather than clobbering the ball.
- Learn to hit a one handed backhand volley: More reach, better touch. And, it's a must when you have to handle a body shot.
- Volleys are gratifying! Learn to enjoy the moment when your opponent runs like it's time for dinner and can't get there in time.

I have one last comment about volleys. Avoid the "Frankenstein volley"! That's the volley you hit with your arm extended straight out. First of all you're grip will be too tight. If you misjudge the ball, you'll find yourself swinging out-to-in, making it extremely hard to place the ball where you want it to go.

Obviously, there might be a situation where the Frankenstein volley is unavoidable, but if that sort of thing happens to you frequently; your footwork is probably the issue. You need to move to the ball. If you don't love to volley, or have trouble ending points, this is your new goal. Having an effective volley makes the game much more enjoyable. And, it will put more pressure on your opponent to go for a low percentage shot.

One-Handed Backhand Volley

A lot of players use two hands even when they are volleying at the net. While I am a huge fan of the two-handed backhand for groundstrokes, I recommend a one-handed backhand when you're at the net. Why? More reach, better touch and more mobility on balls hit right at you.

The set up for this stroke is straightforward. It starts with a continental grip. Place your non-dominant hand on the throat of the racket, using your middle finger or index finger and thumb to brace it. Use that hand to get your body turned and your racket to the side without going behind you. Many players try to do it all with their right hand instead of letting their left hand provide some support.

When you move your racket forward to the ball, your left hand goes back for balance, also pushing your weight forward which should give you more pace without swinging.

Keeping your racket at a consistent angle throughout the stroke is important. Keep your wrist firm and keep the racket face above the net especially when trying to get depth. The arm should ideally be straight. If there is any bend in the elbow, it should only be slight.

I was taught years ago that you should imagine the butt of your racket is on a table so it can't be lowered. It moves through the ball. I think it's a helpful visual, well worth remembering. Some players who transition to a one-handed backhand volley complain about lack of pace. Remember, if you're blowing someone off the court with your volleys then you're probably doing it incorrectly, meaning you're swinging at your volley and your errors will increase.

One question I am asked frequently about the one-handed backhand volley is, "Why wasn't I taught this shot from day one?" At first, most players don't have the wrist strength to support this shot but if you are reading this, I'm sure you've developed it. The more you practice this shot the better other shots will become, including your slice, low and short defensive backhands and even the dreaded high backhand above your shoulder. Years ago, when I transitioned to the one-handed backhand volley, I fought it. Then I started watching a lot of professional tennis. Can you name three pros on tour that use a two handed backhand volley? I can't.

Slice

If topspin is king, slice is your queen. Having an effective slice is a must. It's great for control and it adds variety to your shot selection. To be successful in tennis it's important to vary the pace and type of shots you hit. It keeps your opponent off balance, making it hard for them to develop a rhythm. Another reason to learn this shot is it exposes your adversary's poor footwork. It's also great for defense since it's a shorter swing.

Note that when slice is properly executed, the ball has a backward rotation, which causes the ball to check, keeping the ball low.

There are two grips you can use to hit a slice. One way is with an eastern forehand grip. I don't recommend it though, because you will not be able to impart maximum spin on the ball. The preferred option is the continental grip. It's easier to adjust the racket angle.

How do you hit an effective slice?

1. A good slice shot is hit smoothly.
2. Open the racket face to hit this shot.
3. It should clear the net by six to twelve inches and travel in a straight line. The ball stays low to the ground after bouncing.
4. Start with your racket head high and slowly descend swinging down to the ball and hitting it on its top side. If your ball flight is too high then you may be getting under the ball instead of slowly descending down. Also lean into it to get your weight forward. Keeping your contact point in front of you will also help lower the flight of the ball.
5. The racket should finish slightly on your contact side but no further than the middle of your body, depending on the depth you desire. If your racket finishes below your knee then you may be descending too sharply, i.e.; chopping. If the ball is extremely low, obviously your racket won't start as high and your swing will need to be slower so the ball won't pop up.
6. Follow through; stopping just short of your body's left side.

7. I cannot stress enough the importance of slowing down your swing on this shot when you are first trying to master this shot. If you swing too hard or too fast, you risk losing depth, or worse, hitting the ball into the net. Again, this is not a shot you want to rush.

A few additional points:

Adjusting your racket angle is a key as well, meaning how you lay your wrist back. If it's too open obviously the ball will go sky high. That's why you need to practice this shot so you feel comfortable with your wrist angle.

If your ball moves from left to right make sure your swing path is not going from out to in. It may be fun to see the ball move like this, but it usually slows the ball down more and depth could be an issue. When depth is an issue, check your wrist angle and please slow things down. This shot is not meant to blow someone off the court. It's all about placement.

A slice is great for approach shots because it keeps the ball low, frequently causing your opponent to pop the ball up when they return it. A slice can also be effective on your return of serve, especially when you're facing a player who has a big serve. A slice return in this situation requires a shorter backswing and allows you to use your opponent's pace.

In doubles, this play becomes especially useful when your opponents both play back. Your return pulls the player you hit the ball to into the court; often resulting in a weak return shot putting you on offense. Learn to hit a slice. Be patient. It is a touch shot. I'll make you a bet: Once you master the slice, you'll find that you have more options in developing a point.

The Backhand Slice

The backhand slice is a great shot to change the pace of a rally. It's also an effective approach shot. You can use it to return low balls as well as when you are forced to play defense. This is a great play for those who are tall, or who bend at the waist to hit low balls.

Employing a continental grip, you hold the racket much like the one-handed backhand volley. Your racket face is slightly open. However, take your racket back so the butt of the racket doesn't go past your hip. Much like the one handed volley, use your left hand to stabilize the racket and when bringing it forward to contact the ball, move your non-dominant hand behind you for balance. There is no need to throw your left hand forward for power. The contact point for this shot should be in front of your body.

If you are just beginning to learn this shot, I would start my racket higher than my waist. As you begin to master it you can start your racket high or low depending on the height of the ball, but remember that low equals slow when it comes to racket head speed. Above all, don't rush this shot. Your swing should be a fluid, smooth motion with a shorter follow through than a typical groundstroke. You're not coming up and over your shoulder. The higher you start your racket the more spin you'll impart on the ball. Again, remember to slow down your swing.

Make sure you don't swing out to in, crossing your body on this shot. Swing down and through, not down and across. Your swing is almost parallel to the court.

You know you've hit a good backhand slice when the ball stays low and lands in the last three to four feet of the court. Also the ball's flight should remain fairly straight with very little curve from right to left. If you see your shot curve dramatically, you are moving your racket from in to out. This is not to say that you can't hit it short, but if you do it, your shot better end the point since you've now invited your opponent to the net.

This is a must have shot to become a complete player and much like the serve, you will notice many people struggle with the spin, not the pace.

Shot Making Specialty Shots

A specialty shot is one that serves a very specific purpose and is used strategically.

Inside Out Forehand

Whether you realize it or not, you've hit an inside out forehand; probably more often then you think. Many players would describe this shot as running around your backhand. While accurate to a degree, there's more to it than that.

With this shot, you're hitting a forehand from the ad side of the court (deuce side for lefties.) You make contact with your racket left of the court's center line, i.e., the inside of the court. Your goal is to hit the ball to the outside of your opponent's ad court, trying to make her hit a backhand.

Hitting an inside out forehand allows you to trade a forehand for a backhand stroke which for most players is their preferred option. Another advantage of this stroke is it's the longest court you're going to have, giving you more of a margin for error. It's also a great shot to employ when returning a second serve from the add side of the court. Finally, it's great for generating your own pace during a rally.

How do you hit an inside out forehand effectively?

1. Your set up on this shot is beyond closed, meaning your right foot is well behind your left foot.
2. Footwork however, is different. You have to take many small steps to get to the left side of the ball.
3. You'll want to hit the ball flatter with not as much topspin as you normally do.
4. Hit the ball aggressively! You'll be out of position. Remember your feet will be in, or close to the alley. That leaves a lot of court for your opponent.

The beauty of the inside out forehand is it turns a potentially defensive situation into an offensive opportunity. If you're successfully hitting inside out forehands, you're moving your feet well. If I'm struggling with my backhand, my number of inside out forehands increases. One final thought while we're discussing forehands from the ad court. Although it's a lower percentage shot, hitting the ball down the line once in a while makes it harder for your opponent to anticipate. That shot is known as the inside-in forehand.

Hitting the Ball on the Rise

Hitting on the rise is moving to the ball and striking it early, when it's about waist high. To start doing this effectively, you must shorten your backswing and move into the court. There are four distinct advantages to hitting the ball early.

1. It helps you maintain a better position on the court. For example, if you return a top spin lob on the rise you can avoid being put in a defensive position.
2. It takes time away from your opponent.
3. It's also an effective way to return a kick serve.
4. It makes you less susceptible to the high backhand return.

Hitting the ball on the rise is one of the most difficult things to do. It takes a lot of practice to get the timing right. It is however, very beneficial, especially if hitting high backhands is a struggle.

The Drop Shot

In my experience, very few players know how to hit a drop shot. Before reading any further, visualize yourself hitting one. When I took my USPTA teaching pro exam in Atlanta, I witnessed two players who were also taking the exam, do exactly what I see so many players do. They hit a high-to-low slashing shot to impart spin. Is that what you imagined? You're not alone. I see it all the time. The examiner giving the test took mercy on them and let them try it again after he demonstrated the proper technique.

A drop shot is like a bunt in baseball. Use a continental grip with very loose grip pressure and stick your racket out. There's very little movement if any with your hands, but you still step to the ball as you would with a volley. Again, like a bunt, you must let the ball come to you. Ideally, you want the ball to sink into your racket strings, absorbing the ball. Your racket is positioned near your hip, not farther out in front like the volley.

The golden rule of the drop shot: Never hit the ball into the net. What I'm saying of course, is the ball only has to clear the net by an inch or two. You can use a bit more loft. Practice this shot and you will see you can control's the ball's loft more than you think you can. Remember that even a bad drop shot makes your opponent run.

How do you know you've hit a good drop shot? If the ball bounces twice in the service box, you've done it! If your opponent says, "That was a cheap shot," just say thanks.

The time to hit a drop shot is when your opponent is behind the baseline and you are at least two feet inside the court. A drop shot is an effective way to get them out of their comfort zone. The closer you are to the net, the easier this shot becomes. One caveat to this shot relates to the pace of the incoming ball. The harder the ball is hit the harder it is to execute.

If you notice your opponent is fatigued, hitting more drop shots will win you some points and tire them out even more.

I should add here that a drop shot can become a drop volley if you hit the ball before it bounces. The technique is essentially the same.

Crosscourt Rollover

This shot is one of my all time favorites. The goal is to land the ball short in the court at an angle so that you can take control of the point or even end the point. The crosscourt rollover is one specialty shot you'll definitely want in your arsenal. Using a semi-western or eastern grip, it's a shot where your follow through goes across your body at the waist. Your racket head finishes closer to your hip. Usually, you'll hit this shot from in front of the baseline. You want to hit the side of the ball while brushing up and then rolling over the ball so when you're finished the racket face will be closed. While you can use an open stance, this shot is easier to make with a closed stance. Using a closed stance will allow you to get more hip and shoulder rotation. A great time to employ this stroke is when your adversary has created an angle with their shot.

When you hit this shot, aim for the corner of the service box. As you become more proficient you can attempt to hit at a sharper angle. Top spin helps this shot but it isn't necessary. However, if you aren't using top spin, take some pace off the ball to avoid having it go wide. Not using topspin takes the rollover part out of the shot and will give you less room for error.

If you're looking for an opportunity to take control of a point early, use this shot to return weaker second serves. You'll also put a great deal of pressure on the server to get more first serves in. The crosscourt rollover is also an excellent passing shot. Most passing shots go down the line or, in doubles, down the center of the court. When players shift to the alley and middle to cover their angle, this is a great play for a winner or at least to make them volley below the net.

Hitting a crosscourt rollover will keep your opponent guessing. If you struggle moving your opponents off the court, this is a great shot to add to your game and its fun to practice.

The only warning I have with this shot is some players move well and thrive on angles. When you come across players like this, believe me you'll figure it out quickly.

The Swinging Volley

Like any other volley, the swinging volley is a ball you take out of the air. The big difference is contact point. You take this shot at the waist or higher. Using a semi-western grip to impart topspin on the ball, take a full backswing and follow through, coming straight across your body. You are moving toward the ball as you swing. Hit this shot squarely, driving straight through the ball. The tricky part about this shot is that you can't drastically hit up or down on the ball. While you can hit this shot from anywhere on the court, more often than not you'll take this shot from no-man's land. Since this is a controllable ball, you have options as to where you will hit it. If you have an opening, go for it.

This shot is particularly effective when your opponent is on defense. Say, for example, they've hit a floater or a higher ball to buy time to get back into position. That's an opportunity for you. Also, if you have trouble hitting overheads during your match, you may find that waiting for the ball to come down to shoulder height, then stepping into with a swinging volley, might be a good alternative for you.

For years, I fought teaching this shot, but it is a very important part of today's game. If you don't feel comfortable hitting volleys with a continental grip from anywhere in the court, or you lack topspin, I would recommend getting better at those skills before devoting hours to this shot.

As with most specialty shots, your timing has to be precise and choosing the right ball is critical. Practice will help you make the swinging volley an outstanding weapon.

Master the Half Volley

Think about the best doubles team you have ever faced. I'll bet they were intimidating at the net. But how did they get there? Getting to the net isn't always easy but if you master the half volley, doubles becomes a lot more fun. First of all, what exactly is a half volley? It's a shot you use when your opponent hits the ball at your feet. Use a continental or eastern grip with light pressure. With your hands out in front you push the ball forward. Obviously you are hitting this ball on the rise. It's low and you want to keep it low when you return it. Do your best to hit to the player deepest in the court, returning it in the same direction it came from.

Keep this in mind: If you can return a half-volley with your own half-volley, you are doing it well.

It's not easy and I get a many players that say "How many of these am I really going to hit during a match?" After hearing that question a few times, I decided to count the number of half volleys I hit in a match. It was more than twenty! You're likely to be standing in no man's land when you have to hit this shot. Remember we're not Olympic sprinters. We can't always get from the baseline to the middle of the service box before the next shot gets to us. Still, if you hit two half-volleys in a row you are over your limit! After you hit one you should be moving to the net.

Here are four things you can focus on to improve your half volley:

1. Never go backwards. Going backwards puts your weight on your back foot and the ball tends to float which is not a good thing for you or your partner.
2. Slow your hands down. Fast hands make the ball sit up. You are in a defensive position so your goal here is to keep the ball low.
3. Get your racket low and bend your knees. Starting your racket higher will take too much time and you might gain too much racket head speed.

If you practice these few things and become relentless about your net play you will succeed. Remember you can't win every point. Stay positive and continue to put pressure on your opponents. Good Luck!

Squash Shot

The squash shot is strictly a defensive shot. It's called a squash shot because you use your wrist as you would in a game of squash. Similar to the slice, you use the same grip but you whip at the ball with your wrist, since you're extended and won't be able to generate pace with any other part of your body. When you're taken out wide, your body and racket fully extended, you snap your wrist at the point of contact, hitting the ball crosscourt. Obviously, this is a desperation shot. Beware: if you find yourself having to take this shot often, either you're not moving your feet enough, or you're not getting enough depth on your groundstrokes. This is an advanced shot and you won't use it much. As you develop your game, the squash shot is not a priority.

The Inverted Forehand

Thanks to players like Rafael Nadal, the game is always evolving. The "Buggy Whip" or inverted forehand has been around for years, but is now being used more than ever. Many players don't know this technique by name, but I'm sure you have seen it. It's a forehand that is hit with great topspin and racket head speed, but the finish is on your hitting side up and over your head.

For many years this was a defensive shot, allowing players to put lots of topspin on the ball and giving the ball some height when they got out of position. With the string and racket technology that's available today, some players have equipment that is too powerful and are forced to hit this as their normal shot. I'm not saying this is a bad thing since they are able to harness the power of their equipment, but I worry about the long term affect on the shoulder with this high, helicopter like finish. For very advanced players, I believe this is a must shot, but should not be used every time for the forehand.

Tweener

If you've watched pro tennis for a while, no doubt you've seen this shot. Imagine being close to the net when your opponent throws up a great lob forcing you to turn and run. The ball is so far behind you that you can't outrun it. As you get closer to the boundary of the court you let the ball drop very low and try to hit it between your legs with your back to your opponent. Even when a pro as accomplished as Roger Federer successfully hits a tweener, he can't help but smile. I'm not a fan of the tweener. Still, once you've seen it done, its fun to watch and fun to try. If you pull it off you can talk about it forever. That said, it is the ultimate desperation shot. I have a deal with the players on my high school team. I tell them, "You can hit all the tweeners you want. But if you miss you owe me 50 pushups."

In more than 30 years of playing tennis, I've never lost a point because someone hit this shot. I have, however, won points from my opponent's missing this glorified shot. A final note to the men about this shot: The follow through can be quite painful if your racket winds up in your personal no-man's land. I've seen it happen.

Do You Have a Weapon?

When you reach the point where your game is reasonably consistent, it's time to establish a weapon. What do I mean by a weapon? A weapon is a shot that dictates, or ends the point. Typically, a weapon is a shot with a lot of pace, but pace isn't always necessary.

Common weapons include a big first serve, an aggressive kick or slice serve, inside out forehand, overheads, the swinging volley and even the drop shot. How do you decide which weapon is right for you? Start with the shot you're most comfortable with now. Then think about how often you hit this shot in a match. If it's only once or twice at best, it's probably not worth the time and effort it takes to turn it into a weapon.

In choosing a weapon, recognize that you must practice if you want to perfect it. As you begin to use it in matches, you're going to make mistakes, going for it at the wrong time, improper technique, etc. Don't get discouraged. Keep practicing the shot and don't be afraid to use it during matches. The hard work will pay dividends.

You'll know you have an effective weapon when your opponents adjust their style of play to try to keep you from using it.

For Singles Players Only

What Type of Singles Player Are You?

Singles players come in three types; baseliners, those who serve and volley and all-court players. The baseliner is not afraid of long rallies. He hits the ball deep, often with pace and he has the stamina to do it. The serve and volley player is increasingly rare, but it can still be an effective style. It appeals more to taller players who have a huge "wingspan" to cover the net. Some serve and volley specialists though, struggle moving side to side.

The all-court player is as comfortable at the baseline as he is at the net. This player may serve and volley, but he can also handle a baseline rally. Knowing what type of player you are is important. It allows you to build a strategy designed to take advantage of your strengths. Note that when I talk about your style of play, I'm not suggesting that it's an all or nothing situation. Far from it, I'm simply talking about your preference. You're not confined to one style of play.

In fact, to be successful, there are times when you have to be able to adjust your game. For example, while you may love the baseline, some opponents will be better baseline players than you are. You may find it necessary to come to the net for instance, to disrupt their game and improve your chances. It's worth noting that baseliners tend to be shorter, perhaps because coming to the net is a bit more challenging for them. As I said earlier, taller players can take advantage of their height and wing-span to seek opportunities to come to the net.

If you're not sure what your preferred style is here are some questions for your consideration:

1. Do you have the patience to hit ten or more groundstrokes to win the point?
2. Do you have the stamina for long rallies, or do you need to get to the net to end points sooner?
3. Are your volleys and overheads reliable enough to end points?
4. Can you consistently control your serve placement and pace to improve your chances at the net?

If you answered yes to questions 1 and 2 and no to questions 3 and 4, you probably prefer the baseline. On the other hand, if you said no to questions 1 and 2, and yes to 3 and 4, serve and volley might be your thing. Finally, if you answered yes to all four questions, you may be an all court player.

Three Keys to Successful Singles

1. Increase the height of the ball on your groundstrokes as they go over the net. Unless you have exceptional

racket speed, you want to hit the ball three feet over the net. Hitting the ball higher helps you to achieve better depth, which will keep your opponent at the baseline, playing defense. Achieving proper height above the net may also cause your opponent to shorten up their swing due to a lack of time. If they do that, they'll lose depth on their shot. When this happens, it should give you more opportunities to attack.

2. When hitting a groundstroke, hit the ball crosscourt whenever possible. That way the ball travels over the lowest part of the net. You also have more court space to work with. Going crosscourt makes it harder for your opponent to change the direction of the ball due to the ball's rotation. While changing direction can be an effective tactic, the majority of your shots, as many as 80% of them, should go crosscourt.
3. Get your first serve in! In singles it's critical. Why? Teaching pros tell players to attack the second serve. If your first serve is out, you'll be playing more defense than you want to play. In doubles, there is an opponent obstructing half of the court. In singles, a returner facing a second serve has the entire court to work with.

Court Positioning

Court positioning in singles is radically different than in doubles play. Obviously, in singles you're responsible for covering the entire court. In singles you will rarely stand at the center line in the middle of the court. Most of you were probably taught to return to the middle after you hit each shot. Yet, most balls are hit crosscourt. Going to the middle after each shot will put you on defense. You're constantly running. Eventually, you will wind up wrong footed, or at the very least, leaning in the wrong direction.

Worried about leaving too much of the court open if you stay between the center line and the out of bounds line? Listen, if you hit a good crosscourt ball, the odds that your opponent will successfully change the direction of the ball are long. Of course, if you happen to hit a short controllable ball to your opponent, you may want to move closer to the middle of the court. Where should you stand? The angle of your groundstroke determines where you stand. If you hit a sharp angle shot, stand closer to the alley.

Take control of the baseline. Stand just one foot behind the line to take time away from your opponent. Take a step into the court to hit your groundstroke. Doing that gives your opponent less time to hit a return shot. Keep in mind that if you stand father back behind the baseline, you are opening up the court which makes your opponent's angle more effective. By standing closer to the baseline, you can cut off the angle and make a solid return shot. This is not to say you have to hit every ball on the rise, or you can't back up on a higher deeper ball, but your goal is to not open the court up to your opponent.

Remember that if you play too deep, it becomes much harder to effectively return a short ball. You're running in while the ball is dropping fast, leaving you with the unenviable task of hitting a defensive shot when you should have been on offense.

Improve Your Fitness

If you really want to play singles, you'll quickly discover that just playing matches is not enough for you to be competitive. Singles demands much more from a player than doubles. You're hitting every ball, you're covering the whole court, and as your game improves, rallies tend to last longer. If you're playing someone with similar skills, fitness will often determine the outcome of the match.

If you want to be a successful singles player, you must be willing to combine an off court fitness program with on court drills, working with a coach or a practice partner. Executed properly, you will hit more balls during a drill than you will in a match. Drills are a great way to build stamina, which is critical in a hotly contested match. When you're in shape, you have more confidence that you can outlast your opponent. Being physically fit also helps to make you sharp mentally. A fatigued player is much more likely to make mistakes, go for too much, or try to end the point early.

When it comes to off court conditioning, it's important that you consult with a professional trainer who can help you develop a program that's right for you. Factors such as your general condition at the outset, your goals, your weight, age, etc. are important to review with a trainer.

When to Change the Direction of the Ball

The Wardlaw Directional is a tennis concept introduced by Paul Wardlaw, which put simply, makes it clear that it's always easier to return a crosscourt ball back in the same direction. Tennis is a game that requires patience especially when you play singles. Smart players know they can cut down on unforced errors by hitting the ball crosscourt, which is why they win more matches.

While hitting the ball crosscourt is your preferred shot, obviously you can't always do that. As your game improves you will want to learn to change the ball's direction. Most passing shots for example, are hit down the line. You want to be able to hit the ball to the open court. Sometimes you change the direction of the ball to get out of a forehand to forehand (or backhand to backhand) rally.

What should you look for before you try to change a ball's direction? First, you want a controllable ball, one that is short and doesn't have much pace. When you do change direction, move your target two feet inside the court. In other words the ball doesn't have to hug the sideline for the shot to be effective. It's also important to maintain your balance. Don't lean excessively to one side and be sure to maintain your finish. Notice that if you find you can't hold your finish, chances are you're off balance.

One thing I don't recommend is changing the ball's direction without a specific reason for doing so. Have a strategic reason for doing it.

Know Your Opponent

Some players have a philosophy that goes like this: "I play the same game no matter who my opponent is." Unfortunately, that approach can be fraught with problems. There are times when you must adjust your style of play to be able to take full advantage of your opponent's weaknesses. Sometimes you hear the game referred to as a chess match, as each player makes strategic moves designed to exploit the other player's weakness. Observing your opponent's style and figuring out how to beat them, is one of my favorite things about tennis.

There are four common styles of play. Each one presents opportunities and problems.

The Pusher

This player is the one most of us hate to play. The pusher gets almost every ball back with very little pace. A lot of players knock this style because it isn't fun to watch, but pushers win a lot of matches. Their opponents become frustrated, making high risk shots to end the point.

How do you beat the pusher? Be *very* patient. Anticipate the match taking longer than most matches. Once play begins, look for opportunities to be aggressive. Hit the ball at your pace and look to come to the net more often. Unless you are a pusher, do not make the mistake of slowing down the pace of your shots to match the pusher's pace. Trying to match their style of play will probably result in a long afternoon and typically you will lose.

The All Court Payer

This player tends to be solid in all areas, but doesn't dominate one aspect of the game. The all court player likes the baseline *and* the net. When you're playing an all court opponent, you have to figure out where you are the stronger player. Is it the baseline or at the net? When your opponent is at the net, test her volleys. Can she control them deep or only hit short? When she is at the baseline, how does she handle extra spin? How does she react on the run? Try to force her to play in the area where you excel relative to her.

The Big Hitter

The big hitter usually has a big serve and a big forehand. If this player is allowed to use these weapons, it can be a long day for you. The good news is the longer a rally lasts, the better your chances of winning the point. Big hitters are prone to making unforced errors. Mix up your pace, add spin and keep the ball deep. Getting into long rallies is the way to beat the big hitter. Don't be discouraged if they hit some great shots. Believe me it won't happen the entire match.

The Serve and Volley Player

While the serve and volley style of play isn't as popular as it once was, some players still use it effectively. Obviously, this player typically comes to the net after most serves he hits. He's also constantly looking for opportunities to get to the net. Knowing this player is coming to the net, you must do a few things well. First, use a lot of topspin or slice. This forces the serve and volley player to return a lot of volleys below the net. Second, you have to be willing to lob. Trust me, once your opponent realizes you have a reliable lob they won't be able to close as tightly on the net for easy volleys.

Make them hit the first volley. Serve and volley players often go too big on the return and their unforced errors skyrocket. If someone beats you on a first volley, that's impressive since they will typically be near the service line. Just don't give them the point off the first shot. Also test the forehand volley vs. the backhand. Many serve and volley players have a weaker side. These players are relentless, so there may be a few very short games, but keep plugging away and your opportunities will come. Finally, when you see an opening for a passing shot, be ready and willing to pull the trigger and hit a solid groundstroke by this player.

Drills

Some things you should know about these drills:

1. None of these drills require a tennis pro, or coach to do them effectively.
2. All of these drills should have a scoring component to make the practices competitive.
3. None of the drills confine you to a set position once the point is in play.
4. Be sure to alternate roles throughout practice, especially in situations where only one side is winning.
5. If you're struggling to win a drill, don't get discouraged. View it as a skill that needs more attention.
6. Proper feeding is important to successful drilling. Ideally, feed with a continental grip. If it's not a fair feed, re-feed the ball. As you and your practice partners get better, it's okay to hit more challenging feeds.

Lob Drill

2-4 players

Purpose: This drill allows you to practice hitting volleys and lobs in realistic conditions. Through practice, you should gain more confidence hitting overheads anywhere in the court and improve control of your lobs.

Description:

1. One player(s) start at the net the other at the baseline. If done as a singles drill, the whole court or half of the court may be used.
2. The baseline player feeds the ball to the net player who must hit a volley past the service line to start the point.
3. The baseline player **must** hit a lob after the first volley from the net player.(s)
4. The point is played out to its conclusion.
5. Score is kept until one side has reached four. The winning player(s) start at the net for the next round.

Squeeze Play Drill

2-4 players*

Purpose: Work on half-volley technique and getting out of no-man's land. Players become comfortable in transition by moving forward rather than playing defense. Hand and foot speed as well as touch should also improve.

Description:

1. All players stand between the baseline and the service line, AKA no man's land.
2. One side feeds to the other, so the ball bounces as close as possible to the opponent's feet.
3. Once the point is in play, all players should be moving forward to the net.
4. Points are played out until one side reaches 4.

*For two players, use half the court, either down the line, or crosscourt only.

Jerk feed
2-4 players

Purpose: To work on a quick first step and defensive drills as well as learn how hard and how much spin you can put on a ball without making an error.

Description:

1. Spin to see who will drop feed the first point
2. All players start at the baseline for the beginning of every point
3. The player feeding tries to hit a very challenging feed by using as much pace and/or spin as possible. If there is an error off the feed then a point is awarded to the other team and the other team now feeds

4. The point is played out and the team or player that wins the point continues to feed
5. The drill is played until one player or team reaches 7.

Mini Tennis
2-4 players

Purpose: To learn how to create sharp angles by using very little pace and to learn the different grip pressures involved. Slice is encouraged but topspin can also be used.

Description:

1. Players start behind the service line and they spin to see who will feed first
2. The ball must land in the service boxes and the alley can be used if playing as doubles
3. The ball must bounce and players may hit the ball as hard as they want
4. Score will be kept until 7 is reached and the winning team will feed
5. Advanced players can volley but then they are not allowed to hit the ball hard

Taps
2-4 players

Purpose: To work on closing on the net and learn to slow the ball down when volleying below the net

Description:

1. Player(s) start with one foot on the service line.
2. The team that starts the point must drop feed the ball and have it bounce in their opponent's service box. I encourage the feed to be challenging and deep in the box and returners have to let the feed hit the ground first before playing out the point
3. Once the feed lands in the box and the return is in play, players close to the net and now the whole court can be used. If two players are doing the drill I would suggest using half the court.
4. The drill is played out to 7 and winners feed

4 and Go

2-4 players

Purpose: To work on consistency. Players will also learn that it's rare to end the point early in a rally.

Description:

1. Players start behind the baseline and a spin is used to determine who feeds first.
2. The ball is fed fairly and must be hit 4 times before the point can be played out competitively. If the point ends before four shots then no point is awarded.
3. Players play until five points has been reached and winning players start the feed each point.

4. Advanced: when implementing as a doubles drill each player on the court must hit the ball before it can be played out competitively

Gotta Poach
4 players

Purpose: To get better and more comfortable with poaching. Players will also learn that poaching is a great way to elevate their doubles game, the importance of serve placement and the timing of the poach.

Description:

1. Doubles teams play one game alternating who serves once the game is complete.
2. During the course of the game the serving team must poach at least one time during the game.
3. Using hand signals is not a must but then it must be done verbally before the point starts.
4. Teams can choose to play regular scoring or no add.

3 for a win
2-4 players

Purpose: To work on pressure points and closing out games. Players should learn through this drill not to radically change their style of game when faced with a big point.

Description:

1. Players will start behind the baseline for singles or go one up one back for doubles.
2. A spin will determine who feeds first and after that the winning team will feed.
3. Players or teams are trying to win 3 consecutive points to win one "big point."
4. If three points are not won in a row then the other player or team starts to build on their opportunity to win three in a row.
5. Players or teams play until four "big points" have been won.

College Drill

2-4 players

Purpose: Improve defensive skills. You should use this drill to learn to shorten your swing when returning your opponent's overheads. First, neutralize the point. Then look for an offensive opportunity.

Description:

1. One player or team starts at the net.
2. The other player or team starts at the baseline.
3. A baseline player starts the point by feeding a returnable lob at or close to the other team's service line.
4. The point is played out.
5. The baseline player(s) continue to feed lobs to the net player(s) until one side has 4 points.

6. The baseline player(s) don't get to receive lobs until they beat the net player.(s)

Wimbledon Drill

2-4 players

Purpose: End the point with a volley or overhead. This drill is designed to help you work on your transition game and improve finishing points with overheads and volleys.

Description:

1. All players start behind the baseline.
2. Either side feeds a groundstroke. Thereafter, the winning side feeds.
3. The point is played out with both sides trying to get to the net to volley or hit an overhead.
4. If a player ends the point with a volley or overhead, two points are awarded to the winning team- note that a clean winner is not required.
5. If the point ends any other way, only one point s awarded.
6. The drill is played to 7 points.

Serve Escape Drill

2-4 players

Purpose: Practice holding serve. Players should notice improved first serve percentage, the location of your serve and learn to adjust for different return styles.

Description:

1. One player begins the point by serving. Each point is played out.
2. The player must continue serving until he/she holds serve for 3 consecutive points
3. Players alternate serving.
4. Players have the option of serving on either the deuce or add sides, but I recommend you alternate sides each time it's your turn to serve.

ACKNOWLEDGEMENTS

Robbie McCammon

I would like to express my gratitude to all Coaches who get players started in the game of tennis. In my career, I have been fortunate enough to have two mentors in A.W. Speake and Dennis Covington who have helped me in many aspects of tennis. To my wife, Jennifer and my kids Kate and Patrick, who have given up time to allow me to pursue a career I truly enjoy. My friend and writing partner Len Serafino, who encouraged me to start this project. Without him, I would never have finished. I also want to thank first readers who made important contributions to this book, including, Don Blair, Jill Dillon, Deanne Girouard, Cindy Knapp, Chris Patterson and Pete Collins.

Len Serafino

I want to thank Robbie McCammon for not only teaching me to play tennis, but for constantly encouraging me to improve my game. In working with Robbie to write this book I came to understand the incredible depth of his knowledge of tennis and his commitment to helping others play the game. I also want to join Robbie in thanking the super tennis players who read a draft of Baseline to Baseline and made many useful suggestions. Finally, I want to thank my wife Nancy who encourages my writing and puts up with my absence when I'm working on a project.

ABOUT THE AUTHORS

Robbie McCammon played Division I tennis for Western Kentucky University. He is a USPTA tennis professional, who has been teaching tennis for more than a decade. He's the former number one singles and doubles player, (men's open division) in Tennessee and a high performance USTA coach, as well as a former USTA CTC director. Currently active as a high school coach, he's won multiple high school tennis state championships. He is also a three-time Tennessee, mid-state coach of the year. Robbie frequently works with high level junior players as well as adults, offering private lessons and clinics in Middle Tennessee. This is his first book. Robbie lives in Brentwood, Tennessee with his wife Jennifer and their two children.

Len Serafino is the author of *Sales Talk*, a book that offers a step-by-step guide to effective communication skills for sales professionals. The book has been translated into Chinese and Russian languages. The author of three novels, he has also written articles for healthcare business journals. You can sample Len's writing at www.lenserafino.com. An approved USPTA Recreational Coach, he has coached tennis at both middle school and high school levels. Len lives in Nolensville, Tennessee with his wife Nancy.